Tesla's Drive

Tesla's Drive

A Sustainable Evolution Unveiled

Alina Hazel

UNIEK ENTERPRISES

CONTENTS

INDEX 1

Introduction 3

Chapter 1 7

Chapter 2 19

Chapter 3 35

Chapter 4 50

Chapter 5 64

Chapter 6 78

Chapter 7 92

Chapter 8 107

Chapter 9 122

INDEX

Introduction

Chapter 1: Genesis of a Vision
1.1 Exploration of the early vision of Tesla's founders.
1.2 The inception of the company and its initial goals.
1.3 The audacity of Elon Musk's vision for a sustainable future.

Chapter 2: Engineering Tomorrow
2.1 Evolution of Electric Vehicle Technology
2.2 Overview of Tesla's electric drivetrains.
2.3 Breakthrough innovations in vehicle technology.
2.4 The impact of Tesla's engineering on the automotive industry.

Chapter 3: Beyond Cars: Tesla's Energy Frontier
3.1 Expansion into Energy Products
3.2 Discussion on Tesla's foray into solar panels.
3.3 Powerwall and other energy storage solutions.
3.4 Holistic approach to addressing global energy challenges.

Chapter 4: Driving Autonomously
4.1 Autopilot and Autonomous Driving
4.2 Exploration of Tesla's advancements in autonomous driving.
4.3 Impact on safety and the future of transportation.
4.4 Challenges and controversies surrounding Autopilot.

Chapter 5: Resilience Amid Challenges
5.1 Navigating Business Challenges
5.2 Examination of production hurdles and regulatory obstacles.
5.3 How Tesla faced challenges head-on and evolved.

5.4 The resilience that shaped Tesla's corporate culture.

Chapter 6: Musk's Leadership Odyssey
6.1 Leadership Style of Elon Musk
6.2 Analysis of Elon Musk's leadership principles.
6.3 Decisions that defined Tesla's trajectory.
6.4 The intersection of Musk's vision and corporate culture.

Chapter 7: Financial Rollercoaster
7.1 Tesla's Financial Journey
7.2 Overview of Tesla's financial ups and downs.
7.3 Factors influencing the company's financial standing.
7.4 The unique position of Tesla in the eyes of investors.

Chapter 8: The Road Ahead
8.1 Future Innovations and Market Dynamics
8.2 Speculations on upcoming innovations.
8.3 Anticipation of market dynamics in the electric vehicle industry.
8.4 Consideration of potential challenges and opportunities.

Chapter 9: A Sustainable Tomorrow
9.1 Reflection on Tesla's role in shaping a sustainable future.
9.2 The ongoing transformation driven by Tesla's commitment.
9.3 Closing thoughts on the lasting legacy of "Tesla's Drive."

Introduction

In the fantastic woven artwork of mankind's set of experiences, certain people arise as titans, reshaping the forms of our reality and moving civilization into unfamiliar domains. One such illuminating presence figure in the 21st century was Elon Musk, a visionary business person whose nervy undertakings rose above regular cutoff points. Among his horde adventures, none caught the worldwide creative mind more than Tesla, an organization that became inseparable from the commitment of a reasonable future. Tesla's process addresses a change in perspective in the car business, a seismic development that rises above the simple creation of electric vehicles. It exemplifies a comprehensive vision for feasible living, incorporating energy age, stockpiling, and transportation.

At the core of Tesla's story lies a persistent quest for development and a promise to rocking the boat. The organization's beginning in 2003 denoted the beginning of an upheaval, a takeoff from the settled in standards of the auto area. The customary way of thinking directed that electric vehicles were specialty, unfeasible, and bound for restricted achievement. Nonetheless, Tesla overcame these presumption, arising as a feasible competitor as well as a pioneer that re-imagined the boundaries of what an auto could be.

Key to Tesla's command was the acknowledgment that supportability need not be forfeited for execution. Musk, driven by a steadfast confidence in the critical need to progress away from non-renewable energy sources, left determined to demonstrate that electric vehicles could beat their inward burning partners. The outcome was the Roadster, Tesla's debut offering, which broke assumptions and laid out electric vehicles as in excess of an emblematic gesture to ecological cognizance. It wasn't simply a vehicle; it was an indication of a practical vision that could coincide with extravagance and elite execution assumptions.

As Tesla's impact undulated through the car scene, it reached out past the bounds of the actual vehicle. The organization perceived the reliance of different features of present day living, knowing that maintainable energy arrangements were essential to making an agreeable and strong future. Thus, Tesla extended its extension to include sun powered energy and energy stockpiling, showing a complete comprehension of the unpredictable web interfacing transportation, energy, and the climate.

The presentation of the Powerwall, Powerpack, and Megapack denoted Tesla's introduction to energy capacity, introducing arrangements that rose above the traditional framework foundation. This essential expansion highlighted Tesla's obligation to tending to the foundational challenges intrinsic in conventional energy frameworks, empowering people and organizations to bridle sustainable power and moderate their ecological effect. In doing as such, Tesla re-imagined the boundaries of supportable living as well as effectively engaged shoppers to take part in the bigger account of ecological stewardship.

Past substantial items, Tesla's effect resounded in elusive domains too. The organization turned into an image of insubordination against the inactivity of laid out businesses, testing the idea that progress required split the difference. Musk's proud way to deal with development and hazard taking became significant of another variety of business venture, one unburdened by the apprehension about disappointment and unflinching in its quest for extraordinary change. Tesla's story is as much a demonstration of the force of dauntlessness for what it's worth to mechanical ability.

Critically, Tesla's story unfurls against the setting of an inexorably earnest worldwide requirement for economical arrangements. As environmental change speeds up and natural emergencies pose a potential threat, the basic for significant activity has never been more articulated. Tesla's direction lines up with this goal, situating the organization not only as a corporate element but rather as a vanguard in the battle against environmental change. The story of Tesla is, hence, an impression of the more extensive outlook — a time where development isn't an extravagance however an existential need.

Be that as it may, Tesla's process has not been without its difficulties and discussions. The very daringness that pushed the organization to extraordinary levels additionally pulled in doubt and examination. Creation obstacles, monetary choppiness, and the eccentric idea of the securities exchange became vital parts in Tesla's story. Musk's unfiltered presence via virtual entertainment added layers of eccentricism, transforming the President into a polarizing figure whose words and activities could send shockwaves through worldwide business sectors. The division of Tesla as an influencer and a lightning pole for contention portrays an organization that exists at the crossing point of desire and weakness.

Tesla's impact stretches out past the bounds of its corporate central command in Palo Alto, California. The Gigafactories, decisively situated all over the planet, represent a decentralized way to deal with creation, limiting calculated shortcomings and adding to the monetary rejuvenation of locales hungry for development. These rambling offices, more than simple assembling plants, typify the unmistakable indication of Tesla's obligation to versatility and openness, situating the organization as a worldwide impetus for change.

The development of Tesla is a multi-layered story, winding around together strings of innovation, financial matters, climate, and society. It is an account of persistent development, where every achievement — the Model S, Model X, Model 3, and Model Y — addresses another item send off as well as an essential move in an unpredictable round of chess that Musk plays on the leading body representing things to come. The revealing of the Cybertruck, with its modern plan and exoskeleton, embodies Tesla's readiness to rise above the ordinary, as far as innovation as well as in reclassifying the actual feel of car plan.

As Tesla's electric vehicles turned out to be progressively common on streets around the world, the Supercharger network arose as a basic framework part, reducing worries about range nervousness and giving an unmistakable answer for one of the apparent restrictions of electric vehicles. This obligation to building the fundamental environment for electric portability highlights Tesla's comprehensive methodology, where development isn't restricted to the vehicle yet includes the whole client experience.

Tesla's story additionally meets with more extensive cultural discussions about independence and computerized reasoning. The presentation of Autopilot, Tesla's semi-independent driving framework, situated the organization at the cutting edge of an innovative boondocks where machines are endowed with a rising level of control. The quest for Full Self-Driving (FSD) abilities further brings up issues about the moral ramifications and administrative systems expected for the coordination of independent vehicles into standard transportation.

In equal, Tesla's monetary effect couldn't possibly be more significant. As the organization's market capitalization took off, it turned into a point of convergence for banters about market elements, valuations, and the idea of speculative money management. Tesla's presence on the securities exchange, described by emotional variances and transient ascents, turned into a microcosm of the more extensive monetary scene, mirroring the combination of customary industry and the thriving impact of innovation.

Tesla's account stretches out past the bounds of individual achievement or disappointment; it interlaces with the actual texture of cultural change. The progress from gas powered motors to electric power isn't simply an industry shift; it is a turn point in our aggregate relationship with the climate. The decarbonization of transportation, driven by Tesla's constant quest for charge, is a key part in the bigger methodology to relieve environmental change. As countries wrestle with the basic to lessen fossil fuel byproducts, Tesla's effect on the car area becomes a business story as well as a pivotal section in the more extensive story of worldwide maintainability.

The story of Tesla additionally prompts reflection on the idea of corporate obligation. As the organization turned into a behemoth in the auto and energy areas, questions emerged about its job in molding cultural qualities and needs. Musk's blunt backing for environmentally friendly power and his striking decrees about the existential dangers presented by environmental change situated Tesla as a business element as well as an ethical compass, encouraging people and partnerships the same to defy the squeezing difficulties within recent memory.

Chapter 1

Genesis of a Vision

The beginning of Tesla, the organization that would come to represent the vanguard of maintainable development, follows its foundations to a conversion of visionary standards and mechanical desire. In the mid 2000s, as the auto business gripped to the commonality of gas powered motors, Elon Musk, a South African-conceived business person, imagined a future unshackled from the reliance on petroleum derivatives. Musk, who had previously made a permanent imprint on the tech scene with adventures like PayPal and SpaceX, saw a valuable chance to reform transportation and energy from the perspective of supportability.

The year 2003 denoted a vital second in this excursion, as Musk and a gathering of designers established Tesla Engines (presently Tesla, Inc.) with the nervy objective of demonstrating that electric vehicles couldn't rival customary vehicles however outperform them in execution and attractiveness. The organization's very name given proper respect to Nikola Tesla, the nonconformist designer whose commitments to electrical designing laid the foundation for the jolt of the cutting edge world. This decision was representative, mirroring Tesla's purpose to saddle the soul of development and disturbance exemplified by its namesake.

The Roadster, Tesla's debut creation, disclosed in 2008, filled in as the organization's statement of plan. A smooth, superior presentation sports vehicle, the Roadster opposed winning impression of electric vehicles as languid and utilitarian. All things considered, it thundered onto the scene, testing the thought that manageability came to the detriment of speed and style. The Roadster's electric powertrain, got from lithium-particle battery innovation, conveyed noteworthy speed increase as well as a reach that broke biased restrictions.

However, the Roadster was in excess of an elite presentation electric vehicle. It was a harbinger of a change in perspective, a proclamation that feasible living and state of the art innovation could join flawlessly. The progress of the Roadster established the groundwork for Tesla's climb, demonstrating that there was a business opportunity for electric vehicles that rose above the limited bounds of ecological fans — a market that desired both supportability and thrilling driving encounters.

As Tesla wandered into an unfamiliar area, it confronted impressive difficulties. Suspicion posed a potential threat, and the auto business, profoundly dug in many years of regular practices, respected Tesla with a combination of interest and pretentiousness. Notwithstanding, Musk's immovable assurance and key astuteness moved the organization forward. Tesla's best course of action, the Model S, delivered in 2012, denoted a vital second in the organization's development.

The Model S wasn't simply an electric vehicle; it was a demonstration of Tesla's obligation to pushing limits. With a smooth plan, state of the art innovation, and a reach that outperformed numerous fuel controlled partners, the Model S wasn't only a vehicle; it was an assertion of purpose. It broke predispositions about electric vehicles, demonstrating that they could be comparable to customary autos as well as unrivaled in numerous viewpoints.

The presentation of the Supercharger network additionally tended to one of the central worries restraining the boundless reception of electric vehicles: range tension. By decisively setting Supercharger stations, Tesla gave its clients the capacity to leave on lengthy excursions with the affirmation of helpful, fast charging. This framework venture highlighted Tesla's comprehensive methodology, recognizing that the outcome of electric vehicles was contingent on the actual vehicles as well as on the environment supporting them.

Tesla's development went on with the Model X, a SUV that joined the exhibition of the Model S with the reasonableness and flexibility requested by a more extensive purchaser base. Highlighting particular bird of prey wing entryways and high level security includes, the Model X further set Tesla's situation as a purveyor of electric vehicles as well as state of the art car innovation.

The democratization of electric vehicles turned into a focal principle of Tesla's vision with the presentation of the Model 3 of every 2017. Estimated more moderately than its ancestors, the Model 3 intended to carry electric vehicles to the majority. Its smooth plan, long-range abilities, and Autopilot highlights gathered boundless recognition, driving Tesla into standard awareness.

The Model Y, divulged in 2020, exemplified Tesla's talent for expecting market patterns. As the interest for hybrid SUVs flooded, Tesla answered with a vehicle that flawlessly mixed the properties of the Model 3 with the roominess and utility anticipated from a SUV. The Model Y extended Tesla's item setup as well as supported the organization's flexibility to moving buyer inclinations.

Past the domain of electric vehicles, Tesla's story extended to incorporate energy arrangements. The send off of the Powerwall in 2015 denoted the organization's introduction to private energy stockpiling. This smooth battery pack, intended for home use, planned to upset the manner in which people consumed and put away energy. With the possibility to tackle sun based energy during the day and give power during top interest or blackouts, the Powerwall embodied Tesla's obligation to decentralizing and democratizing energy creation.

For a bigger scope, Tesla's Powerpack and Megapack contributions designated business and utility-scale energy capacity. These items, portrayed by their versatility and effectiveness, tended to the intrinsic discontinuity of sustainable power sources, giving a way to store overabundance energy for use during times of popularity. The reconciliation of energy stockpiling into Tesla's portfolio exemplified the organization's acknowledgment of the interconnected idea of transportation and energy.

As Tesla extended its range, the development of Gigafactories all over the planet became significant of the organization's obligation to versatility. These monstrous assembling plants, decisively situated in different areas, highlighted Tesla's goal to decentralize creation, limiting calculated difficulties and adding to neighborhood economies. The Gigafactory idea addressed something other than proficient assembling; it represented a worldwide change in outlook in the manner in which we produce and consume energy and transportation.

Nonetheless, Tesla's process was not absent any trace of difficulties. Creation delays, monetary obstacles, and suspicion from conventional automakers and energy organizations introduced considerable snags. The very qualities that characterized Musk — his unfiltered correspondence style, his daring commitments, and his public persona — added layers of flightiness to Tesla's account. Musk's cooperations via virtual entertainment, where he frequently sincerely shared his considerations and drew in with the general population, in some cases prompted market vacillations and administrative examination.

The story of Tesla additionally interweaved with more extensive conversations about independence and computerized reasoning. The presentation of Autopilot, Tesla's semi-independent driving framework, denoted a critical stage towards the acknowledgment of completely independent vehicles. This, in any case, delivered moral contemplations, administrative difficulties, and inquiries regarding the cultural status for a future where machines shared control of our streets.

In the monetary domain, Tesla's securities exchange direction turned into a subject of extreme examination. The organization's market capitalization took off to remarkable levels, making it the most significant automaker by market esteem. Tesla's valuation turned into a point of convergence for banters about market elements, speculative financial planning, and the valuation of tech-driven organizations. The stock's unpredictability reflected the exhibition of a solitary organization as well as the moving sands of an industry in the pains of change.

Past the domain of business and innovation, Tesla's story met with the more extensive basic of fighting environmental change. The charge of transportation, led by Tesla, arose as a key part in the worldwide work to diminish fossil fuel byproducts. As countries wrestled with the desperation of progressing away from petroleum products, Tesla's effect reached out past the car area, situating the organization as a central member in the aggregate undertaking to relieve ecological debasement.

Fundamentally, the beginning of Tesla addresses more than the introduction of an organization; it typifies a more extensive story of human inventiveness, natural stewardship, and the constant quest for a manageable future. From the venturesome vision of Elon Musk to the unmistakable items that roll off the creation line, Tesla's process encapsulates the development of a thought into an extraordinary power, testing shows and reshaping the shapes of our mechanical scene. As the world rushes toward a questionable future, Tesla remains as a guide — a demonstration of the conviction that development, when saddled for everyone's benefit, has the ability to introduce another period of plausibility and commitment.

1.1 Exploration of the early vision of Tesla's founders.

The beginning of Tesla, the organization inseparable from supportable development, is established in the early vision of pioneers — a dream rose above the limits of conventional auto thinking. In the mid 2000s, as Elon Musk, close by a gathering of specialists, conceptualized the underpinning of Tesla Engines, their main goal reached out past making simply one more vehicle organization. It was a striking statement that maintainability and superior execution could coincide, testing the predominant idea that electric vehicles were specialty, unreasonable, and coming up short on charm of their gas controlled partners.

Elon Musk, currently an illuminator figure in the tech world with victories like PayPal and SpaceX, imagined a future where humankind wasn't obligated to petroleum products. The name "Tesla," giving recognition to the spearheading creator Nikola Tesla, meant the organization's obligation to bridling the soul of development that had changed the world through electrical designing. The organizers left on an excursion to demonstrate that electric vehicles weren't simply an ecological motion yet a down to earth decision that could rethink the car scene.

The Roadster, disclosed in 2008, denoted Tesla's most memorable substantial move toward understanding this vision. A superior exhibition electric games vehicle, the Roadster blew some minds and displayed the capability of electric impetus.

It wasn't only a vehicle; it was an indication of a dream where maintainability consistently incorporated with extravagance and execution. The Roadster's lithium-particle battery innovation not just tested the impression of electric vehicles as languid yet broken the generalization, giving speed increase and reach that outperformed numerous regular games vehicles.

The progress of the Roadster, both economically and in evolving discernments, laid the foundation for Tesla's ensuing undertakings. It exhibited that there was a market hungry for electric vehicles that couldn't coordinate however surpass the presentation of their inward ignition partners. The Roadster was a crucial evidence of idea, delineating that Tesla's organizers weren't happy with making an electric vehicle for a specialty crowd; they were making way for a significant change in the car business.

With the presentation of the Model S in 2012, Tesla raised its aspirations. The Model S wasn't simply a vehicle; it was a progressive assertion. A regular electric car with a smooth plan and state of the art innovation, the Model S reclassified assumptions for what an electric vehicle could be. It flaunted a striking stylish as well as a reach that tested the impediments of electric vehicles. By consolidating style, execution, and reasonableness, the Model S turned into an image of Tesla's obligation to making electric vehicles helpful on a mass scale.

A urgent component in Tesla's initial vision was tending to the weak spot of electric vehicles — range nervousness. The uncovering of the Supercharger organization, a high velocity charging foundation, was an essential move to dispose of this worry. By decisively putting Supercharger stations, Tesla furnished its clients with the capacity to leave on lengthy excursions with the affirmation of helpful, quick charging. This framework venture exhibited Tesla's foreknowledge, understanding that the outcome of electric vehicles depended on the actual vehicles as well as on a thorough biological system supporting them.

The resulting arrival of the Model X in 2015 exemplified Tesla's capacity to improve past the limits of conventional vehicle plan. An all-electric SUV with particular bird of prey wing entryways, the Model X consolidated reasonableness with state of the art highlights. It displayed Tesla's obligation to offering an assorted scope of vehicles that took special care of various customer needs, growing the venture of electric vehicles into fragments customarily overwhelmed by fuel controlled choices.

In any case, Tesla's initial vision reached out past the extent of vehicles. The organization perceived that genuine manageability required tending to energy creation and utilization at a central level. In 2015, Tesla presented the Powerwall, a private energy stockpiling arrangement. This smooth battery pack expected to upset the manner in which people consumed and put away energy at home. By outfitting sun based energy during the day and giving power during top interest or blackouts, the Powerwall exemplified Tesla's all encompassing way to deal with reasonable living.

As Tesla's item portfolio extended, so did its introduction to bigger scope energy arrangements. The Powerpack and Megapack, intended for business and utility-scale energy capacity, separately, exhibited Tesla's obligation to changing the energy area. These items, versatile and productive, tended to the intrinsic discontinuity of sustainable power sources, giving a way to store overabundance energy for use during times of popularity. Tesla's originators, in investigating these energy arrangements, exhibited a comprehensive comprehension of the unpredictable exchange between transportation, energy, and ecological supportability.

The Gigafactories, great assembling offices decisively situated all over the planet, addressed a critical component in the early vision of Tesla's pioneers. These industrial facilities weren't just about proficient creation; they represented a decentralized way to deal with assembling, limiting strategic failures and adding to nearby economies. The Gigafactories typified Tesla's obligation to versatility, recognizing that the change imagined by the pioneers was a worldwide undertaking that expected a disseminated and versatile assembling framework.

Be that as it may, the excursion was nowhere near smooth. Tesla confronted a flood of difficulties, from creation deferrals to monetary obstacles. The very characteristics that characterized Elon Musk — his unfiltered correspondence style, his aggressive commitments, and his public persona — added layers of intricacy to Tesla's direction. Musk's associations via online entertainment, where he frequently sincerely shared his considerations and drew in with the general population, now and again prompted market changes and administrative examination. The early vision of Tesla's organizers, while unflinching, experienced the cruel real factors of a market and industry hesitant to embrace change.

The story of Tesla likewise met with more extensive cultural conversations about independence and computerized reasoning. The presentation of Autopilot, Tesla's semi-independent driving framework, denoted a huge step towards the acknowledgment of completely independent vehicles. This innovation delivered moral contemplations, administrative difficulties, and inquiries concerning the cultural preparation for a future where machines shared control of our streets. The investigation of independence was a mechanical achievement for Tesla as well as an impression of its organizers' tendency to push the limits of what was viewed as conceivable.

In the monetary domain, Tesla's direction on the securities exchange turned into a subject of extraordinary examination. The organization's market capitalization took off to phenomenal levels, making it the most significant automaker by market esteem. This monetary achievement, nonetheless, achieved forward discusses market elements, speculative financial planning, and the valuation of an organization that rode the universes of auto and innovation. Tesla's valuation reflected the presentation of a solitary organization as well as the developing elements of an industry in the pains of change.

Past the domain of business and innovation, Tesla's story interlaced with the more extensive basic of battling environmental change. The zap of transportation, led by Tesla, arose as a key part in the worldwide work to decrease fossil fuel byproducts. As countries wrestled with the direness of progressing away from non-renewable energy sources, Tesla's effect stretched out past the auto area, situating the organization as a central participant in the aggregate undertaking to moderate natural corruption.

Fundamentally, the investigation of the early vision of Tesla's originators uncovers an embroidery woven with nervy objectives, mechanical development, and a pledge to all encompassing manageability. From the Roadster's leap forward to the Gigafactories molding the fate of assembling, Tesla's process mirrors the development of a thought into an extraordinary power. The originators' vision wasn't bound to making an electric vehicle; it was tied in with rethinking the boundaries of transportation, energy, and cultural qualities. As the story of Tesla unfurls, it fills in as a demonstration of the conviction that a significant vision, when energized by constant assurance and development, has the ability to reshape businesses and move a worldwide shift towards a supportable future.

1.2 The inception of the company and its initial goals.

The beginning of Tesla, Inc. in 2003 denoted the beginning of a groundbreaking excursion that would rethink the auto business' direction. The organization's underlying foundations can be followed back to the vision of its originators, drove by the dauntless Elon Musk. At the hour of Tesla's introduction to the world, Musk was at that point a striking figure in the tech world, having helped to establish PayPal and led the aggressive objectives of SpaceX. Notwithstanding, Tesla addressed an altogether unique boondocks — a bold introduction to the domain of electric vehicles and reasonable energy.

The underlying objectives of Tesla were aggressive and multi-layered. Elon Musk, alongside a gathering of specialists, looked to challenge the overarching incredulity encompassing electric vehicles. The car scene of the mid 2000s was overwhelmed by gas powered motors, and electric vehicles were seen as specialty, restricted by range limitations, and frequently excused as unrealistic for standard use. Musk's vision, be that as it may, was relentless — he pointed to make electric vehicles as well as to change the whole auto worldview.

The principal unmistakable result of Tesla's initial vision was the Roadster, uncovered in 2008. The Roadster was in excess of a simple electric vehicle; it was an image of Tesla's expectation to exhibit that supportability and elite execution were not fundamentally unrelated. Using a lithium-particle battery pack got from state of the art innovation, the Roadster broke predispositions about electric vehicles. Its speed increase and reach outperformed numerous customary games vehicles, demonstrating that electric drive couldn't coordinate yet surpass the presentation of conventional gas motors.

At its center, the Roadster wasn't simply a vehicle; it was an essential move by Tesla to oppose the regular story and lay out a traction in an industry impervious to change. The progress of the Roadster established the groundwork for Tesla's resulting adventures, demonstrating that there was a market hungry for electric vehicles that rose above the limits of prior models and engaged a more extensive customer base.

One of the vital starting objectives of Tesla was to dissipate the idea that electric vehicles were unrealistic for regular use. With the presentation of the Model S in 2012, Tesla took a goliath jump towards accomplishing this goal. The Model S was not only a vehicle; it was a change in perspective in the auto scene. A regular electric car with smooth feel, cutting edge innovation, and a reach that exceeded large numbers of its gas controlled partners, the Model S flagged Tesla's obligation to making electric vehicles commonsense as well as helpful on a mass scale.

Notwithstanding the actual vehicles, Tesla's initial vision included a far reaching way to deal with address the difficulties frustrating the boundless reception of electric vehicles. The uncovering of the Supercharger network in 2012 was an essential move to handle one of the central worries — range tension. By decisively setting Supercharger stations, Tesla gave its clients the capacity to set out on lengthy excursions with the confirmation of helpful, fast charging. This framework speculation featured Tesla's ground breaking approach, perceiving that the outcome of electric vehicles was contingent on the vehicles as well as on a steady and open charging environment.

The resulting arrival of the Model X in 2015 showed Tesla's obligation to advancement past customary vehicle plan. An all-electric SUV with unmistakable bird of prey wing entryways, the Model X mixed reasonableness with state of the art highlights. It displayed Tesla's capacity to enhance its item contributions, taking special care of various buyer needs and extending the venture of electric vehicles into fragments customarily overwhelmed by fuel controlled choices.

Tesla's initial objectives stretched out past the domain of vehicles. Perceiving that genuine manageability required tending to energy creation and utilization, Tesla wandered into the energy area. In 2015, the organization presented the Powerwall, a private energy stockpiling arrangement. This smooth battery pack planned to alter the manner in which people consumed and put away energy at home. By bridling sun based energy during the day and giving power during top interest or blackouts, the Powerwall exemplified Tesla's comprehensive way to deal with supportable living.

Expanding on the progress of the Powerwall, Tesla extended its energy answers for incorporate the Powerpack and Megapack, intended for business and utility-scale energy capacity, separately. These versatile and effective items tended to the irregularity of environmentally friendly power sources, offering a way to store overabundance energy for use during times of popularity. Tesla's introduction to energy arrangements highlighted the's comprehension organizers might interpret the perplexing transaction among transportation and energy in the more extensive setting of natural manageability.

A crucial component in Tesla's initial vision was the development of Gigafactories all over the planet. These monstrous assembling plants, decisively situated in different districts, were something beyond proficient creation offices. They represented Tesla's obligation to versatility and openness, recognizing that the change imagined by the pioneers was a worldwide undertaking requiring a circulated and versatile assembling foundation.

Notwithstanding, Tesla's process was a long way from a smooth direction. The organization confronted a progression of difficulties, going from creation postponements to monetary obstacles. The very characteristics that characterized Elon Musk — his unfiltered correspondence style, his aggressive commitments, and his public persona — added layers of intricacy to Tesla's account. Musk's associations via online entertainment, where he frequently genuinely shared his considerations and drew in with the general population, once in a while prompted market changes and administrative examination. The early vision of Tesla's pioneers, while fearless, experienced the brutal real factors of a market and industry hesitant to embrace change.

The account of Tesla additionally converged with more extensive cultural conversations about independence and man-made brainpower. The presentation of Autopilot, Tesla's semi-independent driving framework, denoted a critical stage toward the acknowledgment of completely independent vehicles. This innovation delivered moral contemplations, administrative difficulties, and inquiries concerning cultural preparation for a future where machines shared control of our streets. The investigation of independence was a mechanical achievement for Tesla as well as an impression of its originators' tendency to push the limits of what was viewed as conceivable.

In the monetary domain, Tesla's direction on the financial exchange turned into a subject of extreme examination. The organization's market capitalization took off to exceptional levels, making it the most significant automaker by market esteem. This monetary achievement, in any case, achieved forward discusses market elements, speculative financial planning, and the valuation of an organization that rode the universes of auto and innovation. Tesla's valuation reflected the presentation of a solitary organization as well as the developing elements of an industry in the pains of change.

Past the domain of business and innovation, Tesla's account interweaved with the more extensive basic of battling environmental change. The zap of transportation, led by Tesla, arose as a key part in the worldwide work to diminish fossil fuel byproducts. As countries wrestled with the earnestness of progressing away from non-renewable energy sources, Tesla's effect reached out past the car area, situating the organization as a vital participant in the aggregate undertaking to moderate natural debasement.

Fundamentally, the beginning of Tesla and its underlying objectives address a urgent section in the tale of current development and supportability. From the venturesome vision of Elon Musk to the unmistakable items and foundation that emerged from that vision, Tesla's initial process encapsulates the development of a thought into an extraordinary power. The organizers' objectives weren't restricted to making an electric vehicle; they expected to reclassify the boundaries of transportation, energy, and cultural qualities. As the story of Tesla unfurls, it fills in as a demonstration of the conviction that a significant vision, when energized by persistent assurance and development, has the ability to reshape businesses and motivate a worldwide shift towards a manageable future.

1.3 The audacity of Elon Musk's vision for a sustainable future.

At the core of Tesla's story lies the daringness of Elon Musk's vision for a practical future. From the commencement of the organization, Musk's desires rose above the conventional limits of business and innovation. His vision wasn't simply about making electric vehicles; it was an intense statement that mankind could, and ought to, graph a course towards manageability, untethering itself from the non-renewable energy source reliance that had characterized the cutting edge period.

Musk's boldness was obvious from the actual decision of Tesla's main goal — to speed up the world's change to practical energy. It was a far reaching objective that stretched out past the restricted bounds of auto development, flagging an aim to catalyze a worldwide shift towards cleaner, more supportable practices. Musk's vision was established from a significant perspective of earnestness, an affirmation of the unavoidable natural difficulties that requested extremist arrangements.

The boldness of Musk's vision became substantial with the presentation of the Roadster in 2008. At the point when electric vehicles were generally consigned to the edges of the car scene, Musk looked to resist the norm. The Roadster wasn't simply an electric vehicle; it was a change in outlook. Musk, driven by a relentless conviction that manageability need not come to the detriment of execution and extravagance, meant to demonstrate that electric vehicles could surpass their fuel partners.

The daringness of Musk's vision emerged in the Roadster's lithium-particle battery innovation. This was not a simple transformation of existing innovation; it was a jump into a strange area. Musk was basically rethinking the condition of what was conceivable with electric powertrains. The Roadster's speed increase and reach broke assumptions, showing the way that electric vehicles could be something other than naturally cognizant — they could be exciting, superior execution machines.

As Tesla's process unfurled, Musk's daringness became inseparable from pushing the limits of what was viewed as feasible. The presentation of the Model S in 2012 was a turning point, for Tesla as well as for the auto business in general.

A regular electric car with a smooth plan, state of the art innovation, and a reach that blew some minds, the Model S was a demonstration of Musk's refusal to adjust to the impediments forced by show.

The dauntlessness of Musk's vision reached out to tending to one of the essential worries repressing the boundless reception of electric vehicles — range uneasiness. With the uncovering of the Supercharger network in 2012, Musk handled this challenge head-on. By decisively putting Supercharger stations, Tesla planned to rethink the idea that electric vehicles were just appropriate for short, neighborhood drives. This bold move flagged a takeoff from gradual upgrades; it was an essential jump, recognizing that for electric vehicles to turn out to be genuinely standard, they should have been suitable for really long travel.

The daringness of Musk's vision likewise appeared in Tesla's attack past vehicles into the domain of energy arrangements. The presentation of the Powerwall in 2015 was an essential second. Musk imagined a future where people could produce, store, and consume their own environmentally friendly power. The Powerwall wasn't simply a battery; it was a progressive idea that meant to decentralize energy creation and engage people to assume command over their carbon impression.

This nervy move into energy capacity extended further with the Powerpack and Megapack, focusing on business and utility-scale applications. Musk's vision included individual supportability as well as a more extensive rebuilding of the energy scene. The versatility and effectiveness of these arrangements showed that Musk was thinking on a fabulous scale, perceiving that the change to feasible energy required complete, enormous scope arrangements.

The dauntlessness of Musk's vision was additionally exemplified in the development of Gigafactories all over the planet. These huge assembling offices weren't just about satisfying the ongoing need for Tesla's items; they were vital interests from here on out. Musk imagined an existence where Gigafactories wouldn't just smooth out creation yet in addition add to the monetary renewal of locales hungry for development. This venturesome way to deal with assembling highlighted Musk's conviction that Tesla wasn't simply a vehicle organization; it was an impetus for more extensive financial and natural change.

In any case, the dauntlessness of Musk's vision was not without its difficulties. The very characteristics that characterized him — his unfiltered correspondence style, his aggressive commitments, and his public persona — added layers of intricacy to Tesla's account. Musk's associations via web-based entertainment, where he frequently openly shared his contemplations and drew in with general society, at times prompted market changes and administrative examination. The dauntlessness that powered development likewise carried with it a degree of unusualness that enraptured suppositions about Musk's initiative style.

The dauntlessness of Musk's vision converged with the more extensive cultural discussion about independence and computerized reasoning. The presentation of Autopilot, Tesla's semi-independent driving framework, denoted a critical stage toward the acknowledgment of completely independent vehicles. While Musk's desire to reshape transportation through independence was obvious, it likewise raised moral contemplations, administrative difficulties, and inquiries concerning the preparation of society for a future where machines shared control of our streets.

In the monetary domain, the boldness of Musk's vision worked out on the securities exchange stage. Tesla's market capitalization took off to uncommon levels, making it the most important automaker by market esteem. This monetary achievement, nonetheless, achieved forward discusses market elements, speculative money management, and the valuation of an organization riding the universes of car and innovation. Musk's vision was reshaping enterprises as well as trying laid out thoughts about market conduct and valuation measurements.

Past business and innovation, the daringness of Musk's vision entwined with the more extensive basic of fighting environmental change. The jolt of transportation, led by Tesla, arose as a key part in the worldwide work to diminish fossil fuel byproducts. Musk's bold conviction that electric vehicles could turn into the prevailing type of transportation was not only a business system; it was a pledge to being a central member in the aggregate undertaking to moderate natural corruption.

Basically, the dauntlessness of Elon Musk's vision for a maintainable future characterizes the center ethos of Tesla. A dream goes past making fruitful items; it is tied in with testing the underpinnings of businesses, reforming cultural standards, and impelling humankind towards an additional maintainable and tough future. Musk's daringness isn't just about accomplishing gradual advancement; it is a source of inspiration, a mobilizing cry to rise above the impediments of the present and embrace the boundless conceivable outcomes of what the future could — and ought to — be. As Tesla's process proceeds, it remains as a demonstration of the groundbreaking force of daring dreams when filled by tireless assurance and development.

Chapter 2

Engineering Tomorrow

The direction of Tesla, Inc. is in a general sense established in the idea of "Designing Tomorrow" — a way of thinking that reaches out past the bounds of auto development to envelop an all encompassing vision of a mechanically progressed and economical future. At the core of this story is the persevering quest for state of the art designing, development, and a promise to reshaping the norm.

The designing ethos that characterizes Tesla's process tracks down its foundations in the bold vision of Elon Musk and his group of specialists. At the point when Tesla Engines was established in 2003, the auto business was dug in a worldview overwhelmed by gas powered motors. Musk, currently an illuminating presence in the tech world, imagined a takeoff from this regular direction. His objective was not only to make a fruitful electric vehicle however to design a total change in outlook in the manner in which society moved toward transportation and energy.

The exemplification of this designing vision surfaced with the presentation of the Roadster in 2008. Tesla's most memorable creation vehicle was not only an electric vehicle; it was a wonder of designing creativity. The Roadster's lithium-particle battery pack, obtained from state of the art innovation, was in excess of a power source — it was an image of Tesla's obligation to pushing the limits of what was conceivable. The specialists at Tesla were not happy with imitating existing innovations; they tried to design a powertrain that reclassified the capability of electric vehicles.

The Roadster's speed increase and reach broke assumptions, demonstrating that electric vehicles couldn't rival fuel controlled partners yet outperform them in execution. This was designing with a reason — a reason that went past the prompt objective of making an attractive item to challenge laid out standards and move the auto business into another time.

The Model S, presented in 2012, further exemplified Tesla's obligation to designing greatness. A regular electric car, the Model S flawlessly mixed execution, reach, and state of the art innovation. The consolidation of elements, for example, Autopilot displayed Tesla's designing ability, pushing the limits of what was viewed as feasible in the domain of independent driving. The Model S wasn't simply a vehicle; it was a material whereupon Tesla's designers painted a dream representing things to come of transportation.

One of the urgent designing accomplishments related with Tesla is the Supercharger organization. Uncovered in 2012, the Supercharger stations were decisively positioned to address a basic concern hindering the far and wide reception of electric vehicles — range uneasiness. The designing test was to make high velocity charging stations as well as to lay out a foundation that consistently incorporated with Tesla vehicles, giving an answer for one of the business' most huge hindrances. This extensive designing drive featured Tesla's ground breaking approach, displaying a comprehension that fruitful electric vehicles required not just state of the art innovation in the actual vehicles yet additionally a complete emotionally supportive network.

The brassy designing vision reached out past vehicles into the domain of energy arrangements. The presentation of the Powerwall in 2015 denoted Tesla's introduction to private energy stockpiling. This smooth battery pack, designed for home use, meant to reform the manner in which people consumed and put away energy. By tackling sun based energy during the day and giving power during top interest or blackouts, the Powerwall exemplified Tesla's comprehensive way to deal with supportable living. It was not only a designing wonder; it was an essential move to reclassify the connection among people and energy utilization.

The designing account extended further with the Powerpack and Megapack, focusing on business and utility-scale energy capacity. These versatile and proficient arrangements tended to the intrinsic discontinuity of environmentally friendly power sources, giving a way to store overabundance energy for use during times of popularity. Tesla's designers weren't simply centered around making items; they were designing answers for the complicated difficulties of changing to an environmentally friendly power future.

The development of Gigafactories all over the planet became symbolic of Tesla's obligation to designing versatility. These enormous assembling plants weren't just about fulfilling the ongoing need for Tesla's items; they addressed a designing way to deal with effectiveness and supportability.

The Gigafactories displayed Tesla's devotion to reclassifying producing processes, limiting natural effect, and adding to neighborhood economies. It was a designing technique that went past the sequential construction system, expecting to change the actual groundworks of how items were made.

Nonetheless, the designing account of Tesla was not without its difficulties. The organization confronted obstructions going from creation deferrals to monetary obstacles. The characteristics that characterized Elon Musk — his unfiltered correspondence style, his aggressive commitments, and his public persona — added layers of intricacy to the designing excursion. Musk's collaborations via online entertainment, where he frequently truly shared his contemplations and drew in with the general population, once in a while prompted market changes and administrative examination. The designing ability of Tesla was not resistant to the erratic elements of the business scene.

The investigation of independence and computerized reasoning additionally featured Tesla's obligation to designing tomorrow. The presentation of Autopilot, Tesla's semi-independent driving framework, denoted a critical stage toward the acknowledgment of completely independent vehicles. This was not just about making an innovative curiosity; it was a designing undertaking with significant ramifications for the eventual fate of transportation. Tesla's designers were at the front of creating frameworks that could rethink the connection among people and machines out and about.

In the monetary domain, Tesla's direction on the securities exchange turned into a subject of extraordinary examination. The organization's market capitalization took off to extraordinary levels, making it the most significant automaker by market esteem. This monetary achievement wasn't simply an impression of Tesla's designing accomplishments; it was a demonstration of the market's affirmation of the groundbreaking capability of the designing vision Musk and his group were executing.

Past the domain of business and innovation, Tesla's designing story entwined with the more extensive basic of fighting environmental change. The charge of transportation, led by Tesla, arose as a key part in the worldwide work to lessen fossil fuel byproducts. Tesla's specialists were not simply making vehicles; they were designing a reaction to a worldwide emergency. The effect of their designing endeavors stretched out past the auto area, situating the organization as a central participant in the aggregate undertaking to relieve ecological corruption.

Fundamentally, the account of "Designing Tomorrow" is woven into the texture of Tesla's personality. An account of venturesome designing vision impelled the organization from the incipient days of the Roadster to the development of Gigafactories and the investigation of independence. A demonstration of the conviction designing greatness isn't just about making items; it is tied in with reclassifying enterprises, pushing the limits of what is viewed as conceivable, and forming a future where manageability and development coincide consistently.

As the designing excursion of Tesla unfurls, it remains as a signal — an update that the genuine commitment of innovation lies in its current accomplishments as well as in its capacity to design a tomorrow that rises above the limits of today.

2.1 Evolution of Electric Vehicle Technology

The development of electric vehicle (EV) innovation remains as a demonstration of the groundbreaking force of development, denoting a significant change in the auto scene. From the early tests with electric drive to the refined electric vehicles of today, the excursion has been one of persistent designing, mechanical forward leaps, and a pledge to manageability. As the world wrestles with the basic to lessen fossil fuel byproducts and change away from petroleum products, the development of electric vehicle innovation arises as a pivotal part in the more extensive story of feasible transportation.

The foundations of electric vehicles follow back to the nineteenth hundred years, when designers and specialists started trying different things with electric drive as a practical method for transportation. In 1837, a Scottish creator named Robert Anderson made quite possibly of the earliest electric carriage, fueled by non-battery-powered essential cells. In any case, it was only after the last 50% of the nineteenth century that critical progressions were made in electric vehicle innovation.

One of the spearheading figures in this early period was Thomas Davenport, an American designer who constructed a limited scale electric vehicle during the 1830s. Davenport's vehicle utilized non-battery-powered batteries and showed the plausibility of electric drive for transportation. Simultaneously, during the 1870s, Sir David Salomon, a physicist living in London, fostered a vehicle with a non-battery-powered electric battery, further adding to the beginning investigation of electric portability.

The late nineteenth century saw the appearance of electric taxicabs in significant urban areas like London and New York. These early electric taxis were functional for metropolitan transportation, offering a tranquil and clean option to their boisterous, fuel controlled partners. Be that as it may, the restricted scope of electric vehicles and the difficulties related with charging framework ruined their inescapable reception.

The turn of the twentieth century denoted a time of serious rivalry between electric, fuel, and steam-controlled vehicles. Electric vehicles acquired prominence for their usability and quiet activity, making them interesting to metropolitan occupants. In 1900, electric vehicles represented around 33% of all vehicles out and about in the US.

The Detroit Electric Vehicle Organization, established in 1907, turned into a noticeable player in the early electric vehicle market. The organization delivered electric vehicles known for their dependability and quality, and its vehicles found favor among wealthy people, including Thomas Edison and Henry Passage.

Notwithstanding, the ascent of fuel controlled vehicles, combined with progressions in gas powered motor innovation, prompted a decrease in the fame of electric vehicles by the 1920s.

For a significant part of the twentieth hundred years, electric vehicles assumed a lower priority in relation to their gas fueled partners. The large scale manufacturing and moderateness of gas vehicles, combined with the growing organization of service stations, cemented the strength of gas powered motor vehicles in the car scene. Electric vehicles, meanwhile, became specialty items, frequently connected with explicit applications like golf trucks and forklifts instead of standard transportation.

The resurgence of interest in electric vehicles started in the late twentieth 100 years, energized by developing ecological worries, progressions in battery innovation, and an acknowledgment of the need to diminish reliance on petroleum derivatives. The late twentieth century saw a progression of improvements that established the groundwork for the contemporary period of electric vehicles.

During the 1990s, General Engines presented the EV1, an all-electric vehicle that accumulated consideration for its smooth plan and natural qualifications. While the EV1 addressed a critical forward-moving step in electric vehicle innovation, restricted reach and high creation costs added to its stopping.

The mid 2000s denoted a defining moment with the foundation of Tesla Engines in 2003. Established by Martin Eberhard and Marc Tarpenning, with Elon Musk joining as a financial backer and executive of the board, Tesla set off on a mission to rethink electric vehicles as elite execution, beneficial machines as opposed to simply earth cognizant other options. The presentation of the Tesla Roadster in 2008 denoted a forward leap in electric vehicle innovation, displaying the potential for electric vehicles to convey both speed and reach without settling on extravagance.

A vital component of Tesla's prosperity was its emphasis on creating state of the art battery innovation. The Roadster used lithium-particle battery cells, a critical takeoff from the lead-corrosive batteries normally utilized in before electric vehicles. Lithium-particle batteries offered higher energy thickness, longer life cycles, and lighter weight, tending to a portion of the vital constraints of prior battery innovations.

The progress of the Tesla Roadster made ready for the advancement of additional available electric vehicles. In 2010, Nissan presented the Leaf, a minimized electric vehicle intended for mass-market request. The Leaf turned into the top of the line electric vehicle overall at that point, featuring the developing acknowledgment of electric vehicles among buyers.

The advancement of electric vehicle innovation further advanced with the presentation of the Tesla Model S in 2012. The Model S exhibited the capacities of electric impetus as well as tested the extravagance car market generally overwhelmed by gas powered motor vehicles. With its smooth plan, long reach, and cutting edge innovation includes, the Model S situated electric vehicles as viable options as well as optimistic decisions.

A basic part of the development of electric vehicle innovation has been the progression in battery innovation. The push for expanded energy thickness, quicker charging times, and decreased costs has been at the front of innovative work endeavors. The boundless reception of lithium-particle batteries, combined with progressing investigation into cutting edge battery sciences, has fundamentally worked on the presentation and moderateness of electric vehicles.

The idea of reach uneasiness, a worry about the restricted driving scope of electric vehicles between charges, has been a point of convergence in the development of electric vehicle innovation. Endeavors to address this worry prompted the advancement of quick charging framework, for example, Tesla's Supercharger organization, and upgrades in battery innovation to expand the scope of electric vehicles. These headways play had a critical impact in upgrading the common sense and comfort of electric vehicles for day to day use and really long travel.

The car business' obligation to electric versatility has been highlighted by the presentation of electric models by customary automakers. Organizations like BMW, Portage, Volkswagen, and others have entered the electric vehicle market, offering a scope of electric vehicles and SUVs to meet the different necessities of buyers. The advancement of electric vehicle innovation has become interlaced with the more extensive industry shift towards supportability and diminished natural effect.

Independent driving innovation has arisen as one more wilderness in the advancement of electric vehicles. Organizations like Tesla have coordinated progressed driver-help frameworks, including highlights like Autopilot, into their electric vehicles. The investigation of independent driving addresses a combination of man-made brainpower, sensor innovation, and electric impetus, with the possibility to rethink the idea of transportation before long.

Government drives and guidelines pointed toward lessening ozone harming substance outflows play had a crucial impact in driving the development of electric vehicle innovation. Motivators, sponsorships, and orders for zero-discharge vehicles have urged automakers to put resources into electric vehicle innovative work. These approach estimates have sped up the arrangement of electric vehicles as well as boosted the extension of charging foundation.

The charge of business vehicles has likewise turned into a point of convergence in the development of electric vehicle innovation. Electric transports, conveyance vans, and trucks are getting momentum as legislatures and organizations look to decrease outflows from the transportation area.

Propels in battery innovation, combined with the potential for lower working expenses and natural advantages, position electric business vehicles as a huge part representing things to come of transportation.

The mix of environmentally friendly power sources into the charging framework has added a layer of manageability to the development of electric vehicle innovation. Charging stations fueled by sunlight based and wind energy add to diminishing the general carbon impression of electric vehicles. This all encompassing methodology lines up with the more extensive objectives of making a cleaner and more maintainable transportation environment.

The interconnectedness of electric vehicles with the energy matrix has led to the idea of vehicle-to-framework (V2G) innovation. V2G empowers electric vehicles to consume energy as well as return overabundance energy to the matrix, giving network adjustment and going about as a dispersed energy asset. This bidirectional progression of energy addresses a change in outlook in the connection among vehicles and the energy framework.

As electric vehicles keep on advancing, developments in materials and assembling processes add to further developing effectiveness and lessening ecological effect. Lightweight materials, like carbon fiber and aluminum, upgrade the energy effectiveness of electric vehicles, while maintainable assembling rehearses expect to limit the environmental impression of the creation cycle.

2.2 Overview of Tesla's electric drivetrains.

The electric drivetrains created by Tesla, Inc. address a zenith in car designing, filling in as a key part for the organization's prosperity and driving the more extensive reception of electric vehicles (EVs). As the world wrestles with the basic to progress away from non-renewable energy sources, Tesla's electric drivetrains stand as a demonstration of the organization's obligation to development, manageability, and the constant quest for greatness.

At the center of Tesla's electric vehicles is the exclusive electric drivetrain, a refined framework that replaces customary gas powered motors with electric engines controlled by cutting edge battery packs. This progressive way to deal with auto impetus plays had a urgent impact in reshaping the view of electric vehicles, dissipating fantasies about restricted reach and execution concerns.

The underpinning of Tesla's electric drivetrain lies in its elite execution electric engines. Dissimilar to conventional fuel motors, electric engines give moment force, conveying a responsive and thrilling driving experience. Tesla's designing group centered around advancing engine effectiveness, bringing about electric vehicles that match as well as frequently outperform the speed increase abilities of their fuel partners.

Tesla's electric drivetrains influence rotating flow (AC) enlistment engines, an innovation that follows its foundations to the spearheading work of Nikola Tesla, the organization's namesake. AC enlistment engines offer a few benefits, including straightforwardness of plan, strength, and high power thickness. The utilization of AC enlistment engines lines up with Tesla's obligation to designing arrangements that focus on execution and effectiveness.

The Model S, presented in 2012, highlighted a back tire drive design with a solitary electric engine. In any case, Tesla's development stretched out past regular plans with the presentation of double engine arrangements in resulting models. The double engine, all-wheel-drive setup, known as "Double Engine All-Wheel Drive" or "D" in Tesla's terminology, turned into a sign of the organization's obligation to execution and wellbeing.

In the double engine design, Tesla coordinates an electric engine at the front and back axles, giving autonomous control and circulation of force. This improves footing and solidness as well as adds to unrivaled taking care of and execution in different driving circumstances. The double engine arrangement turned into a characterizing component of Tesla's Model S, Model X, Model 3, and Model Y, displaying the flexibility and versatility of Tesla's electric drivetrain innovation.

The foundation of Tesla's electric drivetrains is the high level battery innovation that controls the electric engines. Tesla's excursion into electric vehicles started with the improvement of the Roadster, which included a lithium-particle battery pack. The

Roadster's battery pack denoted a takeoff from conventional lead-corrosive batteries utilized in before electric vehicles, offering higher energy thickness and worked on in general execution.

The development of Tesla's battery innovation went on with the presentation of the Model S, which included the momentous "skateboard" engineering. In this plan, the battery pack is coordinated into the floor of the vehicle, making a low focus of gravity that improves steadiness and dealing with. The skateboard design boosts inside space as well as adds to the general security and execution of Tesla's electric vehicles.

A crucial second in the development of Tesla's battery innovation was the Gigafactory drive. Tesla's Gigafactories, decisively situated all over the planet, address monstrous assembling offices zeroed in on delivering batteries and electric drivetrain parts at scale. The Gigafactories highlight Tesla's obligation to adaptability and cost-adequacy, tending to the basic difficulties related with the large scale manufacturing of electric vehicles.

Tesla's battery innovation stretches out past the actual vehicles to incorporate energy stockpiling arrangements. The Powerwall, presented in 2015, is a private energy stockpiling framework that uses a similar battery innovation tracked down in Tesla's electric vehicles. The Powerwall permits property holders to store abundance energy created from sustainable sources, like sunlight based chargers, for use during times of popularity or blackouts.

Expanding on the outcome of the Powerwall, Tesla presented the Powerpack and Megapack, intended for business and utility-scale energy capacity. These versatile arrangements assume a pivotal part in tending to the irregularity of sustainable power sources, giving lattice adjustment, and empowering the productive utilization of clean energy. The combination of battery innovation across the two vehicles and energy arrangements features Tesla's all encompassing way to deal with maintainability and advancement.

Tesla's electric drivetrains are not static substances; they are continually advancing through over-the-air (OTA) programming refreshes. Tesla's capacity to remotely refresh the product of its vehicles has turned into a sign of the organization's obligation to persistent improvement. These updates upgrade execution as well as present new highlights, security enhancements, and improvements to the electric drivetrain.

Independent driving highlights are one more component of Tesla's electric drivetrain innovation. Tesla's vehicles are outfitted with a variety of sensors, cameras, and radar frameworks that give ongoing information to its Autopilot and Full Self-Driving (FSD) abilities. Autopilot empowers semi-independent driving, with highlights, for example, versatile voyage control, programmed path keeping, and programmed path changes.

Full Self-Driving addresses the optimistic objective of accomplishing completely independent driving capacity. While the innovation is still in the formative stage and dependent upon administrative endorsements, Tesla's way to deal with independence has situated its electric drivetrains at the front line of the business' investigation of self-driving innovation. The incorporation of independent highlights addresses an intermingling of man-made brainpower, electric impetus, and network inside Tesla's electric drivetrains.

Charging framework is a basic part of electric vehicle reception, and Tesla has tended to this test with its Supercharger organization. The Supercharger stations, decisively situated along significant travel courses, give rapid charging, permitting Tesla proprietors to leave on lengthy excursions with the confirmation of advantageous charging foundation. The Supercharger network is a demonstration of Tesla's comprehensive methodology, perceiving that the progress of electric vehicles is contingent on the actual vehicles as well as on a steady and open charging environment.

Tesla's electric drivetrains have not been without difficulties and contentions. The organization's Autopilot include has confronted investigation and administrative requests, with worries about the preparation of independent driving innovation and the potential for abuse by drivers. The crossing point of innovation, security, and administrative contemplations highlights the intricacies inborn in the advancement of electric drivetrain capacities.

The monetary elements of Tesla, including its market valuation and stock execution, have added layers of intricacy to the story of Tesla's electric drivetrains. The market's reaction to Tesla's stock, portrayed by unpredictability and speculative exchanging, has started banters about valuation measurements, market elements, and the more extensive ramifications of Tesla's situation at the convergence of the auto and innovation areas.

Past the auto business, Tesla's electric drivetrains converge with more extensive conversations about natural supportability and the worldwide progress to cleaner energy sources. The jolt of transportation, initiated by Tesla, has arisen as a vital part of endeavors to lessen fossil fuel byproducts and relieve environmental change. Tesla's electric drivetrains are necessary to this change, giving a feasible and versatile answer for economical portability.

All in all, Tesla's electric drivetrains address a change in outlook in car innovation, testing laid out standards and speeding up the worldwide progress to practical transportation. From the elite presentation electric engines to the state of the art battery innovation and the reconciliation of independence, Tesla's electric drivetrains encapsulate the combination of designing greatness, development, and a pledge to forming the eventual fate of versatility. As the development of electric vehicles proceeds, Tesla's electric drivetrains stand as an image of what is feasible when bold vision meets tireless designing resourcefulness.

2.3 Breakthrough innovations in vehicle technology.

Advancement developments in vehicle innovation have reliably reshaped the car scene, pushing the limits of what was once considered conceivable and moving the business toward new wildernesses. From early creations that upset portability to contemporary progressions that address ecological worries and reclassify the driving experience, these leap forwards highlight the unique idea of car development.

The commencement of the auto time in the late nineteenth century denoted a great forward leap with the improvement of the gas powered motor. German architect Karl Benz is broadly credited with making the main useful auto, the Benz Patent-Motorwagen, in 1886. Controlled by a gas powered motor energized by gas, this development laid the preparation for the cutting edge auto industry. The gas powered motor turned into the predominant impetus innovation for a significant part of the twentieth hundred years, characterizing the mechanical heart of vehicles and driving worldwide industrialization.

The following huge leap forward in vehicle innovation accompanied the presentation of the mechanical production system by Henry Portage in 1913. The coming of large scale manufacturing methods permitted Passage to create vehicles all the more productively, diminishing expenses and making vehicles open to a more extensive portion of the populace. The Model T, presented in 1908, turned into the main efficiently manufactured vehicle, upsetting the assembling system and molding the layout for the advanced car mechanical production system.

Non-freezing stopping mechanisms (ABS) arose as a leap forward in vehicle wellbeing during the 1960s. Initially produced for airplane, ABS opened up in vehicles during the 1970s. This framework forestalls wheel secure during slowing down, permitting drivers to keep up with guiding control during crisis stops. ABS fundamentally further developed vehicle wellbeing, lessening the gamble of sliding and upgrading generally slowing down execution. Resulting progressions in electronic strength control (ESC) further expanded vehicle wellbeing, giving extra help with keeping up with soundness during cornering and shifty moves.

The 1970s saw the improvement of exhaust systems as a forward leap in addressing natural worries connected with vehicle emanations. Exhaust systems diminish hurtful toxins, like nitrogen oxides and carbon monoxide, by working with compound responses that convert them into less destructive substances. Ordered by guidelines in different nations, exhaust systems became essential to gas powered motor vehicles, adding to cleaner air and moderating the natural effect of auto discharges.

The late twentieth century saw the approach of modernized motor control frameworks, introducing the time of electronic control units (ECUs) and motor administration frameworks. These forward leaps considered exact checking and control of different motor boundaries, enhancing eco-friendliness, discharges, and execution. Electronic fuel infusion (EFI) frameworks supplanted conventional carburetors, offering more exact fuel conveyance and upgrading burning proficiency. The incorporation of electronic frameworks changed vehicles into refined, interconnected machines, laying the basis for the computerized period of auto innovation.

Electric power controlling (EPS) arose as a leap forward in vehicle elements during the late twentieth hundred years. Supplanting conventional water driven power guiding frameworks, EPS utilizes electric engines to help with directing, bringing about more responsive and energy-productive control. EPS frameworks upgrade eco-friendliness, diminish support prerequisites, and make ready for cutting edge driver help frameworks (ADAS) by empowering mix with sensors and control units.

The beginning of the 21st century saw the combination of auto innovation with availability, bringing about the time of brilliant vehicles. Leap forwards in telematics, sensors, and correspondence frameworks prepared for the improvement of cutting edge driver help frameworks (ADAS) and associated vehicle advances. Elements, for example, versatile journey control, path keeping help, and crash evasion frameworks became vital to current vehicles, improving wellbeing and laying the foundation for independent driving abilities.

Mixture electric vehicles (HEVs) arose as a critical leap forward because of the developing worries about eco-friendliness and natural effect. The Toyota Prius, presented in 1997, turned into the primary efficiently manufactured half breed vehicle.

Joining a gas powered motor with an electric engine and battery, HEVs accomplished superior efficiency and diminished discharges. This advanced set up for the more extensive reception of zapped powertrains in the car business.

The leap forwards in vehicle innovation took an extraordinary jump with the presentation of electric vehicles (EVs). Tesla, Inc., established in 2003, assumed an essential part in reshaping discernments about electric vehicles with the send off of the Tesla Roadster in 2008. The Roadster exhibited the potential for elite execution electric vehicles, testing the thought that electric vehicles were inseparable from split the difference. Tesla's prosperity catalyzed the more extensive auto industry's interest in electric impetus innovation.

Headways in battery innovation have been a key part for the far and wide reception of electric vehicles. Lithium-particle batteries, described by high energy thickness and longer life cycles, turned into the prevailing power hotspot for electric vehicles. Forward leaps in battery science, fabricating cycles, and energy stockpiling limit have added to the drawn out range and further developed execution of electric vehicles. The improvement of quick charging foundation, for example, Tesla's Supercharger organization, tended to worries about range nervousness, making electric vehicles more reasonable for day to day use and really long travel.

Independent driving innovation addresses perhaps of the most noteworthy advancement lately. The combination of sensors, cameras, radar frameworks, and man-made brainpower has prepared for vehicles fit for exploring without human intercession. Organizations like Tesla, Waymo, and others have been at the very front of creating and testing independent driving abilities. Albeit completely independent vehicles are still in the trial stage and face administrative obstacles, the advancement in this space implies a change in perspective in store for transportation.

Energy component electric vehicles (FCEVs) have arisen as one more forward leap in elective impetus innovation. FCEVs use hydrogen energy components to produce power, transmitting just water fume as a side-effect. While still in the beginning phases of commercialization, power module innovation holds guarantee for accomplishing zero-outflow transportation and tending to the limits related with battery electric vehicles, for example, charging foundation and reach.

The idea of vehicle-to-everything (V2X) correspondence addresses a leap forward in upgrading the network of vehicles with the more extensive transportation foundation. V2X empowers correspondence among vehicles and components, for example, traffic signals, street signs, and person on foot gadgets. This innovation can possibly further develop traffic stream, upgrade security, and prepare for more effective transportation frameworks.

3D printing, or added substance fabricating, has arisen as an extraordinary leap forward in vehicle producing. The capacity to make unpredictable parts layer by layer offers benefits as far as plan adaptability, diminished material waste, and smoothed out creation processes. Auto makers are investigating 3D printing for prototyping, customization, and in any event, creating basic parts, flagging a shift toward more nimble and maintainable assembling rehearses.

Lightweight materials, like carbon fiber and high level composites, have become advancement developments in vehicle plan. These materials offer a positive solidarity to-weight proportion, adding to further developed eco-friendliness and generally execution. The combination of lightweight materials in vehicle development tends to the double difficulties of lessening ecological effect and upgrading energy productivity.

The idea of vehicle jolt has reached out past traveler vehicles to incorporate business vehicles. Electric transports, trucks, and conveyance vans have arisen as leap forwards in reasonable transportation. Organizations like Tesla, Rivian, and others are spearheading electric business vehicles, adding to the decrease of emanations from the more extensive transportation area.

The leap forwards in vehicle innovation are not restricted to the actual vehicles but rather stretch out to the more extensive foundation that upholds them. Shrewd urban communities and smart transportation frameworks address a dream where vehicles, traffic signals, and street foundation convey flawlessly to streamline traffic stream, improve wellbeing, and diminish blockage. These forward leaps line up with the more extensive objectives of making more productive, practical, and interconnected metropolitan transportation biological systems.

The forward leaps in vehicle innovation are entwined with more extensive cultural and ecological goals. The progress toward cleaner, more maintainable transportation is driven by worries about air quality, environmental change, and the limited idea of petroleum derivatives. Unofficial laws and motivations assume a significant part in forming the heading of car development, empowering makers to put resources into cutting edge innovations that line up with ecological and security objectives.

The crossing point of leap forwards in vehicle innovation with the ascent of the sharing economy has brought about developments in versatility administrations.

Ride-sharing stages, vehicle sharing projects, and the approach of independent taxicabs address forward leaps in rethinking the customary proprietorship and use models .

2.4 The impact of Tesla's engineering on the automotive industry.

Tesla's effect on the car business is downright progressive, reshaping the scene of a deep rooted area through intense designing, mechanical development, and a promise to maintainability. Since its establishing in 2003, Tesla, Inc. has turned into a pioneer in electric vehicles (EVs), independence, and energy arrangements, pushing the limits of what was thought conceivable and testing conventional car standards.

At the core of Tesla's impact is its devotion to designing greatness, a responsibility that became obvious with the presentation of the Tesla Roadster in 2008. This all-electric games vehicle denoted a takeoff from the overarching idea that electric vehicles were restricted to little, utilitarian plans with compromised execution. All things being equal, Tesla displayed that electric vehicles couldn't coordinate however outperform the speed increase and scope of their gas partners.

The Roadster's designing ability laid on the imaginative utilization of lithium-particle battery innovation. Tesla's designers utilized progressions in battery science to make a power-thick and superior execution battery pack, tending to one of the essential worries obstructing the boundless reception of electric vehicles: restricted range. The Roadster's speed increase and great reach rocked the boat, changing impression of electric vehicles and laying out Tesla as an amazing powerhouse in the auto business.

Tesla's effect stretched out past individual vehicles to the making of a complete charging foundation — the Supercharger organization. Divulged in 2012, this organization of quick charging stations addressed one of the main boundaries to electric vehicle reception: range tension. By decisively putting Superchargers along significant travel courses, Tesla gave an answer for charging limits as well as shown a comprehensive way to deal with encouraging electric versatility. This designing accomplishment displayed Tesla's capacity to think past the limits of the actual vehicle and designer arrangements that tended to the more extensive difficulties of electric transportation.

The Model S, presented in 2012, addressed a turning point for Tesla and the car business in general. This standard electric vehicle was a victory of designing, flawlessly mixing execution, reach, and state of the art innovation. The Model S's speed increase, dealing with, and smooth plan dazzled auto fans as well as dispersed waiting questions about the abilities of electric vehicles. Tesla had effectively shown the way that electric vehicles could be sumptuous, strong, and down to earth — all in a solitary bundle.

A significant part of Tesla's effect on the car business is its unfaltering obligation to over-the-air (OTA) programming refreshes. This designing methodology, novel to Tesla, permits the organization to refresh and improve the product of its vehicles from a distance. This empowers bug fixes and execution enhancements as well as presents new highlights and functionalities. The ceaseless improvement worked with by OTA refreshes has turned into a sign of Tesla's designing way of thinking, exhibiting the organization's nimbleness and obligation to conveying progressing worth to its clients.

Independent driving innovation arose as another wilderness where Tesla's designing had an extraordinary effect. The presentation of Autopilot, Tesla's semi-independent driving framework, denoted a huge move toward accomplishing full independence.

While different organizations were likewise investigating independent driving, Tesla's methodology was particular — utilizing a blend of sensors, cameras, and man-made consciousness to empower gradual updates that continuously improved the capacities of Autopilot. This designing procedure situated Tesla at the bleeding edge of the race toward independence, testing customary automakers and tech goliaths the same.

The bold designing vision reached out to the Model X, Tesla's all-electric SUV presented in 2015. This vehicle not just exhibited Tesla's capacity to differentiate its item setup yet additionally displayed designing developments, for example, hawk wing entryways — an element that joined reasonableness with a dash of futurism. The Model X's blend of execution, flexibility, and particular plan additionally cemented Tesla's situation as an industry chief.

The finish of Tesla's endeavors in designing was the presentation of the more reasonable Model 3 of every 2017. This minimal electric car expected to carry electric vehicles to a more extensive customer base. The Model 3 turned into a business achievement, becoming one of the most outstanding selling electric vehicles worldwide. Its effect was felt as far as marketing projections as well as in testing the customary idea that electric vehicles were specialty items. Tesla's designing discernment was instrumental in driving down costs, further developing effectiveness, and democratizing admittance to feasible transportation.

Past traveler vehicles, Tesla's designing wandered into the domain of energy arrangements. The Powerwall, presented in 2015, was a private energy stockpiling framework intended to supplement sunlight based chargers. This designing advancement permitted property holders to store overabundance energy produced during the day for use during top interest periods or in the event of blackouts. The Powerwall exemplified Tesla's all encompassing way to deal with supportability, utilizing designing aptitude to address energy challenges on both the individual and cultural levels.

Tesla's effect on the auto business stretched out to the business area with the presentation of the Tesla Semi in 2017. This all-electric Class 8 truck guaranteed great execution as well as a critical decrease in working expenses contrasted with conventional diesel trucks. The Tesla Semi exhibited the versatility of electric drivetrain innovation to address the issues of business transportation, offering a brief look into a future where long stretch shipping could be both effective and practical.

A basic part of Tesla's designing effect lies in the development of Gigafactories. These enormous assembling offices, decisively situated all over the planet, address a change in perspective in the scale and proficiency of electric vehicle creation. Gigafactories are not just gathering plants; they are designing wonders that enhance fabricating processes, limit ecological effect, and add to the large scale manufacturing of batteries and electric drivetrain parts. The Gigafactory drive highlights Tesla's obligation to versatility, effectiveness, and supportability in its designing practices.

The monetary elements of Tesla additionally mirror its effect on the auto business. Tesla's market capitalization took off to uncommon levels, making it the most important automaker by market esteem. This monetary achievement wasn't simply an impression of Tesla's designing accomplishments; it was a demonstration of the market's affirmation of the groundbreaking capability of the designing vision Musk and his group were executing. The convergence of designing, development, and market elements situated Tesla as a disruptor that constrained conventional automakers to rethink their methodologies and speed up their own zap endeavors.

In any case, Tesla's effect additionally started discussions and debates. The quick ascent in the organization's stock value prompted inquiries concerning market valuations, speculative exchanging, and the maintainability of such market elements. Pundits raised worries about the expected overvaluation of Tesla, featuring the difficulties of exploring a scene where monetary measurements and conventional car benchmarks appeared to separate from market opinion.

Tesla's designing effect isn't bound to its own prosperity however has provoked a more extensive industry shift toward zap. Conventional automakers, once reluctant to completely embrace electric vehicles, sped up their own electric vehicle programs in light of Tesla's prosperity. The business wide obligation to electric portability became obvious with declarations of significant automakers putting vigorously in electric vehicle innovative work, uncovering plans for electric vehicle arrangements, and focusing on transitioning away from gas powered motors. Generally, Tesla's designing effect turned into an impetus for a more extensive change in the auto business.

Tesla's designing accomplishments likewise impacted the extravagance auto market. The outcome of the Model S and resulting models disturbed the thought that extravagance and elite execution vehicles should depend on gas powered motors. Conventional extravagance automakers confronted expanding strain to integrate electric drivetrains and trend setting innovations into their contributions to stay serious in a market where Tesla had set new benchmarks for execution, reach, and development.

Ecological manageability has been a main thrust behind Tesla's designing undertakings. By advancing the reception of electric vehicles, Tesla expected to add to the decrease of worldwide fossil fuel byproducts and moderate the natural effect of transportation. The push toward maintainable energy arrangements, as exemplified by the joining of sunlight based energy items into Tesla's portfolio, mirrors a designing obligation to tending to the more extensive difficulties of environmental change.

All in all, Tesla's effect on the auto business is a demonstration of the force of striking designing, development, and a visionary way to deal with maintainability. From the weighty Tesla Roadster to the mass-market progress of the Model 3, Tesla's designing accomplishments have reshaped the assumptions for what is conceivable in the car world.

The organization's obligation to constant improvement, over-the-air updates, independence, and feasible energy arrangements has situated Tesla as an industry chief as well as has catalyzed a more extensive change inside the car area. As Tesla keeps on pushing the boundary.

Chapter 3

Beyond Cars: Tesla's Energy Frontier

Past its exploring work in the auto area, Tesla, Inc. has left on an extraordinary excursion into the domain of economical energy arrangements, reclassifying the manner in which we create, store, and consume power. Tesla's introduction to the energy boondocks is portrayed by its obligation to address worldwide energy challenges through inventive advances, including sun powered energy, energy capacity, and framework arrangements. This extension lines up with Tesla's all-encompassing mission of speeding up the world's change to reasonable energy.

A significant component of Tesla's energy methodology is sun powered energy, and this responsibility became substantial with the procurement of SolarCity in 2016. Tesla perceived the collaboration between electric vehicles and sun based power, imagining a future where clean energy produced from the sun could control our homes as well as our vehicles. By coordinating sun based energy into its portfolio, Tesla looked to make a comprehensive biological system that tends to both transportation and energy needs.

One of the lead items in Tesla's sunlight based energy setup is the sun powered rooftop. Divulged in 2016, the sunlight based rooftop addresses a change in outlook in sun powered charger style. Dissimilar to customary sunlight based chargers that are mounted on top of existing rooftops, the sun powered rooftop is intended to consistently coordinate with the engineering of a home, serving both as a defensive roofing material and a sun oriented energy generator. The sun based rooftop comes in different styles, imitating the presence of ordinary roofing materials while saddling the force of the sun.

Tesla's sun powered chargers and sun based rooftop influence high-productivity photovoltaic cells to catch daylight and convert it into power. The incorporation of sunlight based energy into private and business structures offers a double advantage: it decreases dependence on customary lattice power and adds to the age of perfect, environmentally friendly power. Property holders can pick to utilize the sun based energy straightforwardly or store it for sometime in the future, making a more manageable and independent energy model.

To supplement its sun based energy contributions, Tesla presented the Powerwall in 2015 — a private energy stockpiling arrangement. The Powerwall is a battery-powered lithium-particle battery pack that stores overabundance energy created by sunlight based chargers during the day for use during times of popularity or when sunlight based creation is low. This capacity tends to one of the critical difficulties of sun oriented energy — irregularity — by giving a dependable and productive method for putting away excess energy for sometime in the future.

The Powerwall isn't restricted to sun based applications; it can likewise be charged from the framework during off-top hours when power rates are lower. This component permits property holders to exploit cheaper power and utilize put away energy during top hours when rates are higher. The flexibility of the Powerwall adds to lattice strength, empowering customers to deal with their energy utilization really and lessening the general burden on the electrical matrix.

Increasing its energy stockpiling arrangements, Tesla presented the Powerpack and Megapack, intended for business and utility-scale applications. The Powerpack, presented in 2015, targets business and modern clients, offering a secluded energy stockpiling framework that can be tweaked to satisfy differing energy needs. The Megapack, presented in 2019, is a much bigger scope arrangement intended for utility-scale projects, giving a gigantic stockpiling ability to balance out the electrical network and backing environmentally friendly power joining.

Tesla's energy stockpiling arrangements reach out past individual homes and organizations to address more extensive network difficulties. The Hornsdale Power Save project in South Australia, highlighting Tesla's Powerpacks, acquired worldwide consideration for its capacity to give quick reaction network administrations. The task exhibited the capability of energy stockpiling to upgrade lattice dependability, further develop unwavering quality, and work with the reconciliation of environmentally friendly power sources.

Notwithstanding its sun oriented and energy capacity items, Tesla has wandered into lattice arrangements with the improvement of the Autobidder stage. Autobidder is an ongoing exchanging and control stage that empowers Tesla's energy stockpiling frameworks to take part in power markets. This stage advances the worth of put away energy via independently dispatching it to the network during times of appeal or when power costs are positive. Autobidder addresses a creative way to deal with network the board, utilizing man-made brainpower and AI calculations to improve the productivity and monetary feasibility of energy stockpiling resources.

Tesla's energy attempts are not restricted to fixed applications; they reach out to electric vehicles also. The reconciliation of energy arrangements into electric vehicles lines up with Tesla's vision of making a far reaching environment where vehicles add to the strength and maintainability of the energy network. This vision is exemplified by

Tesla's V2G (vehicle-to-framework) innovation, an idea that permits electric vehicles to consume energy as well as return overabundance energy to the matrix.

The interconnectedness of Tesla's energy items and electric vehicles adds to the production of an all encompassing energy environment. For example, a Tesla vehicle with bidirectional charging capacity can act as a versatile energy stockpiling unit, permitting proprietors to store overabundance energy from their sun powered chargers or the network in the vehicle's battery. This put away energy can then be utilized to drive the home or be taken care of once more into the network during top interest periods.

The development of Tesla's energy wilderness stretches out past individual customers and organizations to incorporate utility-scale projects. Tesla has been engaged with enormous scope energy capacity arrangements, like the establishment of the world's biggest lithium-particle battery in Hornsdale, South Australia. These utility-scale projects feature the versatility and flexibility of Tesla's energy arrangements, exhibiting their capability to address the difficulties of matrix steadiness and sustainable power joining for an enormous scope.

Tesla's effect on the energy area isn't bound to equipment alone; it stretches out to programming and advanced arrangements. Tesla's energy items, including sunlight based chargers, Powerwall, Powerpack, and Megapack, are coordinated with the Tesla Energy programming stage. This product empowers clients to screen and deal with their energy utilization, creation, and capacity progressively. The easy to use interface gives experiences into energy use designs, permitting customers to enhance their energy utilization and boost the advantages of environmentally friendly power sources.

Tesla's overall objective is to make a supportable energy future, and this vision incorporates a progress toward electric portability past private vehicles. The Tesla Semi, an all-electric Class 8 truck, addresses Tesla's entrance into the domain of economical cargo transport. Past the natural advantages of energizing shipping, the Tesla Semi consolidates energy-proficient highlights and the potential for independent driving capacities, further lining up with Tesla's more extensive vision for a cleaner and more productive transportation biological system.

The effect of Tesla's energy boondocks reaches out to the more extensive energy industry, impacting the talk around clean energy and supportability. Tesla's outcome in exhibiting the practicality of sun based energy, combined with energy capacity arrangements, has prodded revenue and interest in sustainable power projects around the world. States, organizations, and utilities are progressively perceiving the job of dispersed energy assets, energy capacity, and savvy network arrangements in making a stronger and manageable energy foundation.

Nonetheless, Tesla's energy aspirations are not without difficulties and discussions. The versatility of specific energy arrangements, like the sun powered rooftop, has confronted obstacles connected with creation limit and cost-adequacy. Joining with existing network foundation and administrative systems likewise presents intricacies that require cautious route. As Tesla keeps on pushing the limits of energy advancement, these difficulties highlight the complexities of changing the energy scene.

Tesla's effect on the energy business is interlaced with its more extensive mission of supportability, and this responsibility stretches out to tending to ecological worries past individual energy items. Tesla has made significant interests in Gigafactories, decisively situated all over the planet, to create batteries at scale. The Gigafactories not just add to the large scale manufacturing of electric vehicles yet in addition assume a significant part in propelling energy stockpiling arrangements and supporting environmentally friendly power drives.

The ecological effect of Tesla's energy arrangements is apparent in the decrease of ozone depleting substance emanations related with sustainable power age and electric transportation. By empowering buyers to tackle sun oriented energy, store it productively, and power electric vehicles with clean power, Tesla adds to the decarbonization of both the energy and transportation areas. This ecological center lines up with worldwide endeavors to moderate environmental change and progress to a more supportable energy worldview.

All in all, Tesla's introduction to the energy boondocks addresses a visionary obligation to tending to worldwide energy challenges through imaginative designing and manageable arrangements. From sun powered energy and energy stockpiling to network arrangements and electric vehicles, Tesla's arrangement of energy items mirrors a comprehensive way to deal with making a cleaner, stronger energy environment. The effect of Tesla's energy attempts reaches out past individual purchasers to impact the more extensive energy industry, forming the talk around clean energy and manageability. As Tesla keeps on pushing the limits of energy advancement, its job in speeding .

3.1 Expansion into Energy Products

Tesla's venture into energy items addresses a key and visionary move past its beginnings as an electric vehicle (EV) producer. Established in 2003 with the mission to speed up the world's change to supportable energy, Tesla, Inc. has developed into a complex energy organization, expanding its impact from the car area to the more extensive energy scene. This extension is described by an exhaustive set-up of items and administrations intended to reform how we create, store, and consume energy.

At the very front of Tesla's venture into the energy area is its emphasis on sun oriented energy arrangements. Perceiving the critical job of perfect and environmentally friendly power in accomplishing manageability objectives, Tesla took a huge action in 2016 with the obtaining of SolarCity — a main sun based energy administrations organization.

This essential securing permitted Tesla to coordinate sun oriented energy age flawlessly into its portfolio, making a collaboration between sun based power and electric vehicles.

A critical sign of Tesla's obligation to sun powered energy is the sun based rooftop. Disclosed in 2016, the sun based rooftop addresses an earth shattering way to deal with coordinating sun powered chargers into the actual texture of a structure. Dissimilar to customary sun powered chargers mounted on top of existing rooftops, the sun based rooftop is intended to supplant ordinary roofing materials, really transforming the whole surface into a sun oriented energy generator. This development joins feel with usefulness, furnishing property holders with an economical and outwardly engaging material arrangement.

The sunlight based rooftop utilizes high-effectiveness photovoltaic cells implanted in solid glass tiles. These cells catch daylight and convert it into power, outfitting sun oriented power while consistently mixing into the engineering plan of the home. The sun oriented rooftop comes in different styles, from finished to smooth, imitating the presence of conventional roofing materials. This plan flexibility upgrades the allure of sun powered energy, making it an essential piece of home development instead of an extra element.

Tesla's introduction to sun powered energy isn't restricted to the sun oriented rooftop. The organization offers conventional sunlight based chargers intended for retrofitting onto existing rooftops, giving a versatile answer for mortgage holders hoping to outfit sun oriented power without supplanting their whole material design. Tesla's sun powered chargers brag high proficiency and sturdiness, and they are joined by a scope of inverters and energy observing frameworks to upgrade energy creation and utilization.

To supplement its sunlight based energy age capacities, Tesla presented the Powerwall in 2015 — a private energy stockpiling arrangement. The Powerwall is a battery-powered lithium-particle battery pack intended to store overabundance energy created by sun powered chargers during times of daylight for use during seasons of popularity or when sun based creation is low. This tends to one of the critical difficulties of sun powered energy — irregularity — by giving a solid and productive method for putting away excess energy for sometime in the future.

The Powerwall isn't restricted to sun based applications; it can likewise be charged from the lattice during off-top hours when power rates are lower. This component permits mortgage holders to exploit cheaper power and utilize put away energy during top hours when rates are higher. The flexibility of the Powerwall adds to lattice versatility, empowering purchasers to deal with their energy utilization successfully and diminish their dependence on the electrical network.

Growing past private applications, Tesla presented the Powerpack in 2015 — a bigger scope energy capacity arrangement intended for business and modern clients. The Powerpack coordinates different lithium-particle battery packs into a solitary unit, giving a versatile energy stockpiling framework that can be redone to satisfy fluctuating energy needs. This arrangement tends to the difficulties of network security, top interest the board, and irregular sustainable power sources at a bigger scope.

Expanding on the progress of the Powerpack, Tesla presented the Megapack in 2019 — a utility-scale energy capacity arrangement intended for huge scope projects.

The Megapack is a significantly bigger scope variant of Tesla's energy stockpiling innovation, offering an enormous stockpiling limit reasonable for supporting network tasks, improving lattice strength, and working with the coordination of environmentally friendly power sources on a modern scale.

Tesla's utility-scale energy capacity arrangements have been sent in different tasks universally, displaying the adaptability and flexibility of the innovation. Outstanding establishments incorporate the Hornsdale Power Hold project in South Australia, where Tesla's Powerpacks assumed a critical part in balancing out the electrical matrix and giving fast reaction framework administrations. These ventures show the capability of enormous scope energy capacity to change framework the executives and backing the progress to a cleaner and more reasonable energy foundation.

Notwithstanding energy age and capacity, Tesla has wandered into framework arrangements with the improvement of the Autobidder stage. Autobidder is a continuous exchanging and control stage that empowers Tesla's energy stockpiling frameworks to take part in power markets. This stage improves the worth of put away energy via independently dispatching it to the network during times of popularity or when power costs are ideal. Autobidder addresses a creative way to deal with lattice the board, utilizing man-made brainpower and AI calculations to improve the productivity and financial suitability of energy stockpiling resources.

Tesla's venture into energy items isn't restricted to equipment alone; it stretches out to programming and advanced arrangements. Tesla's energy items, including sunlight based chargers, Powerwall, Powerpack, and Megapack, are incorporated with the Tesla Energy programming stage. This product empowers clients to screen and deal with their energy utilization, creation, and capacity continuously. The easy to use interface gives experiences into energy utilization designs, permitting shoppers to improve their energy utilization and amplify the advantages of environmentally friendly power sources.

Past individual buyers and organizations, Tesla's energy aspirations incorporate enormous scope utility activities. The organization has been associated with significant energy projects that influence its energy stockpiling answers for upgrade framework strength and backing the coordination of sustainable power sources.

These utility-scale organizations highlight the capability of Tesla's energy items to assume a pivotal part in reshaping the energy scene on a more extensive scale.

One outstanding model is the development of the world's biggest lithium-particle battery in Hornsdale, South Australia. Dispatched in light of a far reaching power outage in 2016, the Hornsdale Power Save project includes Tesla's Powerpacks and has been effective in balancing out the framework, offering subordinate types of assistance, and exhibiting the feasibility of huge scope energy capacity arrangements. The progress of the Hornsdale project has prompted expanded interest in comparative organizations worldwide, flagging a shift toward stronger and practical energy framework.

Tesla's venture into energy items isn't without difficulties and discussions. The adaptability of specific energy arrangements, like the sunlight based rooftop, has confronted obstacles connected with creation limit and cost-adequacy. Joining with existing lattice foundation and administrative structures additionally presents intricacies that require cautious route. As Tesla keeps on pushing the limits of energy advancement, these difficulties highlight the complexities of changing the energy scene.

Tesla's effect on the energy area isn't restricted to equipment and programming arrangements; it reaches out to the more extensive talk around clean energy and maintainability. By effectively exhibiting the suitability of sun powered energy, combined with energy capacity arrangements, Tesla has impacted the story around the job of environmentally friendly power in moderating environmental change. The organization's accomplishments have prodded revenue and interest in environmentally friendly power projects all around the world, moving state run administrations, organizations, and utilities to investigate economical energy arrangements.

The reconciliation of Tesla's energy items with its electric vehicles addresses a thorough way to deal with making a practical energy environment. The bidirectional charging capacities of specific Tesla vehicles empower them to consume energy as well as return overabundance energy to the framework — an idea known as vehicle-to-matrix (V2G) innovation. This interconnectedness adds to the production of an all encompassing energy biological system, where energy age, stockpiling, and utilization are flawlessly incorporated.

Tesla's overall objective is to make a maintainable energy future, and this vision incorporates a progress toward electric portability past private vehicles. The Tesla Semi, an all-electric Class 8 truck, addresses Tesla's entrance into the domain of reasonable cargo transport. Past the ecological advantages of jolting shipping, the Tesla Semi integrates energy-effective highlights and the potential for independent driving capacities, further lining up with Tesla's more extensive vision for a cleaner and more proficient transportation biological system.

The ecological effect of Tesla's energy arrangements is apparent in the decrease of ozone depleting substance discharges related with sustainable power age and electric transportation. By empowering buyers to outfit sun based energy, store it effectively, and power electric vehicles with clean power, Tesla adds to the decarbonization of both the energy and transportation areas. This ecological center lines up with worldwide endeavors to moderate environmental change and progress to a more reasonable energy worldview.

3.2 Discussion on Tesla's foray into solar panels.

Tesla's introduction to sunlight based chargers denotes a critical section in the organization's main goal to speed up the world's progress to supportable energy. Past upsetting the auto business with electric vehicles, Tesla, Inc. perceived the essential job that sunlight based energy could play in making a comprehensive and environmentally friendly power biological system. The organization's venture into sunlight based chargers lines up with its general vision of a future fueled by spotless, environmentally friendly power sources.

One of the vital minutes in Tesla's excursion into sun oriented energy was the obtaining of SolarCity in 2016. SolarCity, established by Elon Musk's cousins, Lyndon and Peter Rive, was one of the biggest sun powered energy administrations organizations in the US. The procurement permitted Tesla to incorporate sunlight based energy age consistently into its portfolio, making collaborations between sun oriented power and electric vehicles. This essential move flagged Tesla's obligation to turning into a complete energy organization, tending to both transportation and power age.

The Tesla sun powered chargers, intended for private use, address a vital part of the organization's sun based energy contributions. These sun powered chargers influence photovoltaic (PV) innovation to change over daylight into power, furnishing property holders with a perfect and environmentally friendly power source. The plan and proficiency of Tesla's sunlight powered chargers mirror the organization's devotion to consolidating supportability with style, making sun oriented energy an alluring and vital piece of private engineering.

Tesla's sun powered chargers come in different plans and arrangements to take care of various stylish inclinations and energy needs. The smooth and low-profile plan of the boards intends to flawlessly incorporate into the current design of a home, staying away from the cumbersome appearance frequently connected with conventional sun oriented establishments. This plan theory mirrors Tesla's obligation to making sun based energy harmless to the ecosystem as well as outwardly engaging and available.

The productivity of Tesla's sunlight based chargers is a basic figure their allure. High-effectiveness sun powered chargers catch more daylight and convert it into power, expanding energy creation.

Tesla's utilization of cutting edge PV innovation guarantees that its sunlight based chargers are among the most effective on the lookout, permitting property holders to produce greater power with a more modest impression of sun powered chargers on their rooftops.

An outstanding element of Tesla's sun powered chargers is their sturdiness. Built with safety glass, these boards are intended to endure brutal weather patterns, including hailstorms and weighty snow loads. The strong form guarantees that Tesla's sun powered chargers have a long life expectancy, furnishing property holders with a dependable and low-upkeep sustainable power arrangement.

Tesla has zeroed in on the equipment viewpoint as well as acquainted imaginative funding choices with make sunlight based energy more available. The presentation of sun powered memberships and sun oriented credits empowers property holders to take on sunlight powered chargers with decreased forthright expenses, making the change to environmentally friendly power all the more monetarily attainable. These monetary arrangements line up with Tesla's central goal to democratize practical energy and make it open to a more extensive scope of purchasers.

To supplement the sunlight powered chargers, Tesla offers the Sun based Inverter, a critical part of the sun oriented energy framework. The inverter changes over the immediate flow (DC) power created by the sunlight based chargers into exchanging flow (AC), which is utilized to control home devices and can be taken care of once again into the electrical framework. The Sun powered Inverter is intended to boost energy creation and further develop generally speaking framework productivity, guaranteeing that property holders can capitalize on their sunlight based chargers.

Tesla's way to deal with sun oriented energy isn't restricted to individual homes; it reaches out to business and modern applications also. Tesla offers sun oriented answers for organizations, permitting business properties to outfit the force of the sun to meet their energy needs. The adaptability of Tesla's sun powered arrangements empowers organizations to redo sun oriented establishments in view of their energy utilization, adding to maintainability objectives while possibly diminishing functional expenses.

The establishment cycle of Tesla's sunlight powered chargers is a basic part of their openness. Tesla Energy Counsels, prepared experts who guide clients through the whole cycle, assume a significant part in making the change to sun powered energy consistent. From site evaluation to establishment, these consultants guarantee that the sun powered chargers are ideally situated for most extreme daylight openness, improving energy creation proficiency.

Tesla's sun powered chargers are supplemented by the Tesla application, which furnishes property holders with continuous experiences into their sun oriented energy creation and utilization.

The application permits clients to screen their energy age, track the exhibition of their sunlight powered chargers, and evaluate the general effect on their energy bills. This degree of straightforwardness enables property holders to effectively draw in with their energy use and pursue informed choices to streamline their sun oriented speculation.

In spite of the various benefits and advancements related with Tesla's sun powered chargers, the organization has confronted difficulties and contentions in this endeavor. One striking test has been the versatility and creation limit of the sunlight based rooftop — an item that intends to consistently coordinate sun powered chargers into roofing materials. The aggressive objective of making a sun based coordinated rooftop has experienced delays and calculated obstacles, prompting inquiries regarding the inescapable reception of this innovation.

Furthermore, Tesla's obtaining of SolarCity, while basic to its venture into sun oriented energy, has been dependent upon analysis and legitimate examination. A few investors raised worries about likely irreconcilable circumstances, given the familial ties between Elon Musk and SolarCity's pioneers. The fights in court that followed scrutinized the reasonable level of effort and decency of the obtaining, highlighting the intricacies of combining various aspects of the feasible energy industry.

In the more extensive setting of the sun powered industry, Tesla faces rivalry from both conventional sun based organizations and new contestants. The sun based energy market is dynamic, with various players offering different items and administrations. While Tesla brings its image strength, development, and vertical reconciliation to the table, it works in a scene where administrative structures, government motivators, and market elements can impact the achievement and reception of sun oriented innovations.

Tesla's drive into sunlight based energy likewise meets with strategy contemplations and the advancing scene of energy guidelines. Government motivations, tax breaks, and steady strategies for environmentally friendly power assume a critical part in boosting customers to embrace sunlight based arrangements. Changes in government approaches, either steady or prohibitive, can fundamentally affect the financial reasonability and reception pace of sunlight based chargers, influencing Tesla's market situating.

The reconciliation of sun based energy into Tesla's more extensive environment is clear in its electric vehicles (EVs) too. The bidirectional charging capacities of specific Tesla vehicles, known as vehicle-to-lattice (V2G) innovation, empower them to consume energy as well as return overabundance energy to the framework. This interconnectedness adds to the making of a comprehensive energy biological system, where energy age, stockpiling, and utilization are flawlessly coordinated.

The achievement and effect of Tesla's introduction to sun powered chargers go past individual establishments; they add to a more extensive story around the job of sustainable power in fighting environmental change. Tesla's obligation to maintainability and clean energy lines up with worldwide endeavors to diminish fossil fuel byproducts and progress to an all the more harmless to the ecosystem energy worldview. As the organization proceeds to advance and address difficulties in the sun based energy area, its effect on forming the fate of sustainable power stays significant.

3.3 Powerwall and other energy storage solutions.

Tesla's introduction to energy capacity arrangements, exemplified by the Powerwall, addresses an essential move toward reshaping how we produce, store, and consume power. Past changing the auto business with electric vehicles, Tesla, Inc. perceived the basic job that energy capacity plays in making a more maintainable and strong energy environment. The Powerwall, alongside other energy stockpiling arrangements, remains as a demonstration of Tesla's obligation to giving creative and versatile innovations that engage shoppers to outfit the force of environmentally friendly power.

Key to Tesla's energy stockpiling setup is the Powerwall, a battery-powered lithium-particle battery pack intended for private use. Revealed in 2015, the Powerwall tends to one of the key difficulties related with environmentally friendly power sources — discontinuity. While sunlight based and wind energy age are dependent upon variances in light of weather patterns, the Powerwall empowers clients to store overabundance energy during times of high creation for use during seasons of low or no creation, giving a solid and persistent power supply.

The Powerwall's conservative plan houses a high-limit battery fit for putting away power created by sun powered chargers, or it very well may be charged from the framework during off-top hours when power rates are lower. The flexibility of the Powerwall permits mortgage holders to improve their energy utilization, lessening reliance on the lattice during top hours when power costs are regularly higher. This adds to cost investment funds as well as improves by and large framework flexibility.

Key to the Powerwall's viability is its consistent joining with sun oriented energy frameworks. When matched with sunlight based chargers, the Powerwall structures a far reaching private energy stockpiling arrangement. During the day, sunlight based chargers produce power, and the abundance energy not promptly consumed by the house is put away in the Powerwall. At night or during times of low sunlight based creation, the put away energy is then used to drive the home, diminishing dependence on matrix power.

Tesla's way to deal with the Powerwall reaches out past equipment to incorporate inventive funding choices, making energy stockpiling more open to a more extensive crowd. The presentation of sun oriented memberships and sun based credits empowers mortgage holders to take on the Powerwall with decreased forthright expenses, lining up with Tesla's main goal to democratize manageable energy and make it monetarily doable for a more extensive scope of purchasers.

The Powerwall isn't simply an independent item; it is a critical part of Tesla's more extensive vision for energy strength and supportability. The interconnectedness of the Powerwall with sun based energy frameworks, electric vehicles, and the more extensive energy matrix epitomizes Tesla's all encompassing way to deal with making a more effective and feasible energy environment.

Increasing its energy stockpiling arrangements, Tesla presented the Powerpack in 2015 — a bigger scope energy capacity framework intended for business and modern applications. The Powerpack expands upon the standards of the Powerwall yet for a bigger scope, furnishing organizations and utilities with a measured and versatile answer for address differing energy requests.

The Powerpack coordinates various lithium-particle battery packs into a solitary unit, making a higher-limit framework reasonable for bigger establishments. This versatility permits organizations and utilities to alter the size and design of the Powerpack in light of their particular energy prerequisites. The Powerpack's capacity to store a lot of energy makes it a significant device for overseeing top interest, adjusting environmentally friendly power age, and improving generally speaking matrix dependability.

Expanding on the outcome of the Powerpack, Tesla presented the Megapack in 2019 — a much bigger scope energy capacity arrangement intended for utility-scale projects. The Megapack addresses a gigantic jump away limit, making it appropriate for huge scope energy capacity ventures and network level applications. The secluded plan of the Megapack works with quick organization, smoothing out the coordination of energy stockpiling into utility-scale foundation.

Tesla's utility-scale energy capacity arrangements have earned worldwide respect for their part in upgrading matrix dependability and supporting the reconciliation of sustainable power sources. One prominent model is the Hornsdale Power Hold project in South Australia, where Tesla's Powerpacks assumed a urgent part in balancing out the electrical framework. The outcome of such undertakings features the extraordinary capability of huge scope energy capacity in reshaping the elements of matrix the board.

The Autobidder stage addresses one more component of Tesla's energy stockpiling methodology. Autobidder is an ongoing exchanging and control stage that empowers Tesla's energy stockpiling frameworks, including Powerpacks and Megapacks, to partake in power markets. The stage enhances the worth of put away energy via independently dispatching it to the lattice during times of appeal or when power costs are ideal. Autobidder use computerized reasoning and AI calculations to improve the effectiveness and monetary feasibility of energy stockpiling resources, adding to a more powerful and responsive energy network.

The effect of Tesla's energy stockpiling arrangements stretches out past the conventional limits of energy age and utilization. The bidirectional charging abilities of specific Tesla vehicles, known as vehicle-to-matrix (V2G) innovation, empower them to consume energy as well as return abundance energy to the framework. This interconnectedness adds to the formation of a comprehensive energy biological system, where energy age, stockpiling, and utilization are flawlessly coordinated.

While Tesla's energy stockpiling arrangements have earned recognition for their creative methodology and exhibited progress in different undertakings, they are not without difficulties and debates. The adaptability of specific energy arrangements, particularly at the private level, has confronted obstacles connected with creation limit and cost-viability. Incorporation with existing network foundation and administrative structures presents intricacies that require cautious route.

3.4 Holistic approach to addressing global energy challenges.

Tesla's comprehensive way to deal with tending to worldwide energy challenges remains as a spearheading model that rises above customary limits, incorporating electric vehicles as well as energy age, stockpiling, and utilization. Established on the vision of speeding up the world's progress to feasible energy, Tesla, Inc. has left on a diverse excursion that incorporates imaginative innovations, environmentally friendly power arrangements, and a promise to natural maintainability.

At the core of Tesla's all encompassing energy system is a guarantee to perfect and environmentally friendly power age. The organization's introduction to sunlight based energy, set apart by the procurement of SolarCity in 2016, represents this responsibility. Tesla's sunlight based energy arrangements, including sun powered chargers and the progressive sun oriented rooftop, mean to alter the manner in which we produce power for homes and organizations.

The sun oriented rooftop, uncovered in 2016, rethinks the style of sun powered energy. Not at all like customary sun powered chargers mounted on top of existing rooftops, the sun oriented rooftop is intended to altogether supplant ordinary roofing materials. This inventive methodology flawlessly coordinates sunlight based chargers into the actual design of a structure, transforming the whole rooftop into a sun oriented energy generator. The sun based rooftop comes in different styles, emulating the presence of customary roofing materials while outfitting the force of the sun.

Tesla's sun powered chargers, intended for both private and business applications, influence high-proficiency photovoltaic cells to catch daylight and convert it into power. The joining of sunlight based energy into the texture of structures, whether through sun powered rooftops or traditional sun powered chargers, addresses a change in outlook by they way we contemplate energy age. It changes structures from detached purchasers of energy to dynamic supporters of the energy network, lining up with Tesla's vision of making a decentralized and economical energy environment.

Supplementing its sunlight based energy arrangements, Tesla has wandered into energy capacity with items like the Powerwall, Powerpack, and Megapack. The Powerwall, presented in 2015, is a private energy stockpiling arrangement that permits property holders to store overabundance energy produced by sunlight based chargers. This put away energy can be utilized during times of low sun based creation or high energy interest, giving a dependable and persistent power supply. The Powerpack and Megapack stretch out this energy stockpiling ability to business and utility-scale applications, empowering organizations and utilities to oversee top interest, improve lattice strength, and coordinate environmentally friendly power sources flawlessly.

The interconnectedness of Tesla's energy age and capacity arrangements reaches out past individual homes and organizations to incorporate network arrangements. Tesla's Autobidder stage, acquainted with advance the worth of put away energy, empowers its energy stockpiling frameworks to partake in power markets. This constant exchanging and control stage influence computerized reasoning to independently dispatch put away energy to the lattice during times of appeal or ideal power costs. This imaginative methodology upgrades the productivity of energy stockpiling resources, adding to a more unique and responsive energy matrix.

Tesla's comprehensive energy approach reaches out to electric vehicles (EVs), a foundation of the organization's main goal to decarbonize transportation. Tesla's arrangement of electric vehicles, including the Model S, Model 3, Model X, and Model Y, has reclassified the car business as well as assumes a urgent part in the more extensive energy environment. The bidirectional charging abilities of specific Tesla vehicles, known as vehicle-to-framework (V2G) innovation, empower them to consume energy as well as return abundance energy to the matrix.

This bidirectional progression of energy makes a harmonious connection between Tesla vehicles and the energy network. When left, Tesla vehicles can go about as versatile energy stockpiling units, permitting proprietors to store overabundance energy from their sunlight powered chargers or the network in the vehicle's battery. This put away energy can then be utilized to drive the home, got back to the network during top interest periods, or used to charge the actual vehicle. The incorporation of electric vehicles into the energy environment addresses a change in outlook, changing vehicles from simple purchasers of energy to dynamic supporters of lattice solidness.

Past the domains of energy age, stockpiling, and electric vehicles, Tesla's all encompassing methodology stretches out to energy programming arrangements. The Tesla Energy programming stage incorporates with Tesla's energy items, giving clients continuous bits of knowledge into their energy utilization, creation, and capacity. This easy to use interface engages customers to screen and deal with their energy use really, enhancing the advantages of sustainable power sources.

Tesla's comprehensive energy methodology lines up with more extensive worldwide endeavors to address environmental change and progress to a more practical energy future. The reconciliation of environmentally friendly power sources, energy capacity, and electric portability makes a synergistic biological system that goes past the traditional storehouses of the auto and energy businesses. This coordinated methodology lessens fossil fuel byproducts as well as improves energy versatility, lattice solidness, and the general productivity of the energy framework.

The effect of Tesla's all encompassing energy approach isn't restricted to its own prosperity; it has catalyzed a more extensive industry shift toward maintainability. Customary automakers, once reluctant to completely embrace electric vehicles, sped up their own electric vehicle programs in light of Tesla's prosperity. The more extensive obligation to electric versatility became clear with declarations of significant automakers putting vigorously in electric vehicle innovative work, disclosing plans for electric vehicle arrangements, and focusing on eliminating gas powered motors. Generally, Tesla's comprehensive energy technique has turned into an impetus for a more extensive change in both the car and energy areas.

Nonetheless, Tesla's comprehensive methodology isn't without difficulties and contentions. The fast ascent in the organization's stock value prompted inquiries regarding market valuations, speculative exchanging, and the supportability of market elements. Pundits raised worries about the possible overvaluation of Tesla, featuring the difficulties of exploring a scene where monetary measurements and customary auto benchmarks appeared to wander from market feeling.

Tesla's comprehensive energy approach additionally faces administrative and strategy challenges. The versatility of specific energy arrangements, like the sun oriented rooftop, has confronted obstacles connected with creation limit and cost-viability. Combination with existing matrix foundation and administrative systems presents intricacies that require cautious route. Changes in government approaches, either strong or prohibitive.

Chapter 4

Driving Autonomously

Tesla's excursion into the domain of independent driving imprints an earth shattering section in the development of auto innovation. The vision to make vehicles fit for exploring the streets without human mediation has been a longstanding objective in the car business, and Tesla, Inc. has arisen as a leader in this pursuit. The organization's Autopilot and Full Self-Driving (FSD) capacities address a striking introduction to the fate of transportation, consolidating state of the art equipment, refined programming, and a pledge to pushing the limits of what is conceivable in the realm of independent driving.

At the center of Tesla's independent driving abilities is the Autopilot framework. Presented in 2015, Autopilot is a high level driver-help framework that use a mix of cameras, ultrasonic sensors, radar, and man-made reasoning to empower semi-independent driving. The framework was a critical jump forward in auto innovation, presenting highlights like versatile voyage control, path keeping help, programmed path changes, and self-stopping.

Autopilot's versatile journey control keeps a set speed however can consequently conform to match the speed of more slow traffic, guaranteeing a protected and effective driving experience on thruways. Path keeping help utilizes cameras to distinguish path markings and helps keep the vehicle inside its path. Programmed path changes permit the vehicle to move to another lane independently when the driver initiates the blinker. These highlights addressed a stage towards robotization, upgrading driver comfort and security.

Expanding upon the groundwork of Autopilot, Tesla presented the Full Self-Driving (FSD) bundle. FSD is a high level driver-help framework that means to accomplish full independence, empowering the vehicle to explore and work with practically no human information.

While the expression "Full Self-Driving" recommends total independence, it is crucial for note that starting around my last information update in January 2022, FSD isn't completely independent, and Tesla vehicles furnished with FSD actually require driver management and mediation.

The turn of events and arrangement of Autopilot and FSD depend intensely on Tesla's equipment suite, prominently the Autopilot Equipment 3.0 (HW3) PC. This hand crafted chip is enhanced for handling the huge measure of information produced by Tesla's sensors and cameras progressively. The equipment redesign was a significant part in improving the computational capacities of Tesla vehicles, giving the establishment to further developed independent driving highlights.

One of the vital components of Tesla's way to deal with independent driving is over-the-air (OTA) programming refreshes. Tesla vehicles are intended to get programming refreshes from a distance, permitting the organization to improve and grow the capacities of Autopilot and FSD persistently. This capacity to refresh the product of thousands of vehicles all the while empowers Tesla to emphasize on its independent driving highlights quickly, presenting new functionalities and tending to impediments.

In spite of the critical progressions, the excursion towards completely independent driving has not been without difficulties and contentions. The General public of Car Architects (SAE) characterizes levels of driving mechanization from Level 0 (no ro- botization) to Even out 5 (full computerization). Starting around my last information update, Tesla's Autopilot and FSD are by and large viewed as at Level 2 robotization, where the vehicle can deal with a few driving undertakings however requires steady driver oversight.

Debates encompassing Tesla's Autopilot framework frequently rotate around epi- sodes where drivers have abused or misconstrued the capacities of the innovation. A few drivers have been accounted for participating in hazardous way of behaving, like watching films or resting, while the vehicle was working in Autopilot mode. These episodes feature the difficulties of guaranteeing client understanding and capable utilization of semi-independent frameworks.

The administrative scene for independent driving is one more area of intricacy. Various districts and nations have shifting guidelines and norms for the arrange- ment of independent vehicles. Tesla has confronted examination from administrative specialists, and questions have been raised about the wording utilized, for example, the utilization of "Full Self-Driving," and whether it might actually misdirect drivers about the real abilities of the framework.

Tesla's Autopilot and FSD have gone through persistent refinement and im- provement through various programming refreshes. Improved highlights incorporate Explore on Autopilot, which empowers programmed driving on assigned parkways, including path changes and thruway exits. Tesla vehicles furnished with FSD like- wise have the capacity for "Brilliant Gather," permitting the vehicle to independently explore through parking areas to get the driver.

One of the aggressive elements prodded by Tesla is the ability for completely independent "Robotaxi" activity. The thought is that Tesla vehicles, when not being used by their proprietors, could work independently as a component of a ride-sharing armada. While this idea holds guarantee for the fate of metropolitan portability, it likewise raises complex administrative and wellbeing contemplations, as sending completely independent vehicles for public transportation includes a more significant level of investigation and responsibility.

Tesla's Autopilot and FSD have collected both energy and wariness inside the auto business and the more extensive public. Defenders feature the potential for expanded street wellbeing, decreased gridlock, and improved availability for people with portability challenges. Be that as it may, pundits express worries about the restrictions of current innovation, the requirement for more clear correspondence about framework abilities, and the potential dangers related with overreliance on semi-independent elements.

Starting around my last information update in January 2022, the independent driving scene is dynamic, with progressing headways and conversations inside the business. Different organizations, including customary automakers and innovation goliaths, are putting vigorously in independent driving innovative work. The race toward accomplishing more elevated levels of independence isn't restricted to Tesla alone, and rivalry in this space is driving advancement across the car area.

Tesla's Autopilot and FSD venture likewise entwines with the more extensive talk on the cultural effect of independent vehicles. Inquiries regarding position dislodging for proficient drivers, changes to transportation framework, and the moral contemplations of programming decision-production into independent frameworks are indispensable to the bigger discussion about the fate of portability.

It's essential to take note of that the turn of events and sending of independent driving advances include specialized difficulties as well as complicated moral, legitimate, and cultural contemplations. The shift toward independent vehicles addresses a groundbreaking crossroads throughout the entire existence of transportation, with suggestions that stretch out past the auto business.

4.1 Autopilot and Autonomous Driving

Tesla's Autopilot and Independent Driving innovations address an earth shattering endeavor into the eventual fate of car transportation. As a trailblazer in electric vehicles, Tesla, Inc. has played a lead job in propelling the capacities of semi-independent driving elements and trying towards full independence. The improvement of Autopilot, the presentation of Full Self-Driving (FSD), and the constant refinement through over-the-air programming refreshes have situated Tesla at the very front of the independent driving upheaval.

The excursion started in 2015 with the presentation of Tesla's Autopilot — a set-up of cutting edge driver-help highlights intended to improve vehicle security and give a semi-independent driving experience. Autopilot consolidates a variety of sensors, including cameras, ultrasonic sensors, and radar, with complex programming calculations to empower highlights, for example, versatile voyage control, programmed path keeping, programmed path changes, and self-stopping. These highlights denoted a huge step towards facilitating the driver's responsibility and improving the general driving experience.

Versatile voyage control, a basic component of Autopilot, permits the vehicle to keep a set speed while naturally changing its speed to match more slow traffic ahead. This upgrades security and decreases driver weariness, especially during long roadway ventures. The programmed path keeping highlight uses cameras to recognize path markings and assists the vehicle with remaining inside its path. Moreover, Autopilot's capacity to consequently switch to another lane when the driver enacts the blinker adds to the accommodation and ease of expressway driving.

Tesla's Autopilot framework utilizes continuous information from its sensors and depends on AI calculations to work on its exhibition over the long haul. The framework gains from the aggregate driving experience of Tesla vehicles, with every vehicle going about as an information point adding to the improvement of a more modern and skilled independent driving framework. This consistent educational experience, worked with by over-the-air programming refreshes, permits Tesla to emphasize on Autopilot's capacities and acquaint new highlights with the current armada of vehicles.

The presentation of Autopilot started both energy and discussion inside the car local area and among the overall population. Fans commended the potential for expanded street security and the possibility of a more pleasant and tranquil driving experience. In any case, doubters and wellbeing advocates communicated worries about the impediments of the innovation and the potential for driver smugness or abuse.

In light of the advancing scene of independent driving, Tesla presented the Full Self-Driving (FSD) bundle. FSD addresses a high level driver-help framework with a definitive objective of accomplishing full independence — a vehicle fit for exploring and working with no human intercession. The FSD bundle expands upon the establishment laid via Autopilot, presenting extra elements and functionalities that plan to carry Tesla vehicles closer to accomplishing Level 5 independence, as characterized by the General public of Auto Architects (SAE).

The equipment that supports Tesla's Autopilot and FSD capacities is a significant part of their usefulness. Tesla's vehicles are furnished with a set-up of sensors, including cameras, ultrasonic sensors, and radar, that give a far reaching perspective on the vehicle's environmental elements.

A vital part of Tesla's equipment is the specially crafted Autopilot Equipment 3.0 (HW3) PC, acquainted with upgrade the handling power and computational capacities of Tesla vehicles.

The Autopilot HW3 PC is streamlined for the requests of handling the immense measure of information produced by Tesla's sensors progressively. This redesign was a critical achievement in the improvement of Tesla's independent driving capacities, empowering more modern brain organizations and quicker handling speeds. The equipment upgrades, joined with the iterative programming refreshes, add to the general advancement of Tesla's independent driving innovation.

The iterative idea of Tesla's way to deal with independent driving is maybe best exemplified by its obligation to over-the-air (OTA) programming refreshes. Tesla vehicles are intended to get programming refreshes from a distance, permitting the organization to send enhancements, bug fixes, and new elements to its whole armada at the same time. This ability has demonstrated significant in refining and growing the capacities of Autopilot and FSD without requiring actual visits to support focuses.

While Autopilot and FSD certainly stand out and recognition for their development, they have likewise been dependent upon investigation and discussion. High-profile occurrences including Tesla vehicles working in Autopilot mode and mishaps where the framework might have been involved have started banters about the innovation's security and the requirement for more clear correspondence with respect to framework constraints.

The General public of Auto Designers (SAE) characterizes levels of driving robotization, going from Level 0 (no computerization) to Even out 5 (full mechanization). Starting around my last information update in January 2022, Tesla's Autopilot and FSD are for the most part viewed as at Level 2 mechanization. Level 2 mechanization suggests that the vehicle can deal with specific driving undertakings, like directing and speed increase, yet requires steady driver management. Accomplishing more significant levels of robotization, particularly full independence, presents complex specialized, administrative, and cultural difficulties.

The advancement of independent driving innovations includes specialized intricacies as well as administrative contemplations. Various districts and nations have changing guidelines and principles for the organization of independent vehicles. Tesla has experienced administrative examination, and questions have been raised about the wording utilized, for example, the utilization of "Full Self-Driving," and whether it might actually delude drivers about the real capacities of the framework.

The actual wording has been a disputed matter and conversation inside the business and among controllers. The utilization of terms like "Full Self-Driving" can make assumptions that the innovation is further developed than its ongoing abilities.

Overseeing client assumptions and guaranteeing that drivers comprehend the restrictions of the innovation are basic parts of sending independent driving highlights dependably.

Tesla's excursion into independent driving likewise meets with the more extensive talk on the cultural effect of independent vehicles. Inquiries concerning position relocation for proficient drivers, changes to transportation framework, and the moral contemplations of programming decision-production into independent frameworks are necessary to the bigger discussion about the eventual fate of versatility.

Tesla's Autopilot and FSD advancements have gone through ceaseless refinement and improvement through various programming refreshes. Upgraded highlights incorporate Explore on Autopilot, which empowers programmed driving on assigned interstates, including path changes and roadway exits. Tesla vehicles outfitted with FSD additionally have the ability for "Shrewd Call," permitting the vehicle to independently explore through parking garages to get the driver.

The idea of completely independent "Robotaxi" activity has been prodded by Tesla, where Tesla vehicles, when not being used by their proprietors, could work independently as a feature of a ride-sharing armada. While this idea holds guarantee for the eventual fate of metropolitan portability, it likewise raises complex administrative and wellbeing contemplations, as sending completely independent vehicles for public transportation includes a more elevated level of investigation and responsibility.

Starting around my last information update in January 2022, the scene of independent driving is dynamic, with continuous progressions and conversations inside the business. Different organizations, including conventional automakers and innovation monsters, are putting vigorously in independent driving innovative work. The race toward accomplishing more significant levels of independence isn't restricted to Tesla alone, and contest in this space is driving development across the car area.

4.2 Exploration of Tesla's advancements in autonomous driving.

Tesla's steady quest for advancement has situated the organization at the cutting edge of the car business' development toward independent driving. The excursion into independent capacities has been set apart by persistent progressions, from the presentation of the historic Autopilot framework to the continuous improvement of Full Self-Driving (FSD) highlights. Tesla's investigation of independent driving addresses a strong endeavor into an unknown area, testing ordinary thoughts of vehicle activity and reshaping the scene of transportation.

The underpinning of Tesla's investigation into independent driving was laid with the presentation of the Autopilot framework in 2015. Autopilot, as a high level driver-help framework, was intended to upgrade vehicle security and proposition a semi-independent driving experience.

The framework integrated a refined sensor suite, including cameras, ultrasonic sensors, and radar, furnishing the vehicle with a thorough perspective on its environmental elements. These sensors, combined with Tesla's obligation to over-the-air (OTA) programming refreshes, framed the foundation of a dynamic and developing independent driving stage.

Autopilot's underlying highlights included versatile voyage control, permitting the vehicle to keep a set speed while changing in accordance with the speed of encompassing traffic. Path keeping help used cameras to identify path markings and supported keeping the vehicle inside its assigned path. Moreover, Autopilot presented highlights like programmed path changes and self-stopping, denoting a huge jump towards semi-independent driving capacities.

What put Tesla's Autopilot aside was its way to deal with information assortment and AI. Tesla vehicles furnished with Autopilot were not simply inactive beneficiaries of updates; they became dynamic supporters of the advancement of independent driving abilities. The armada's aggregate driving information, anonymized and painstakingly totaled, filled in as a preparation dataset for Tesla's brain organizations. This constant educational experience permitted the framework to improve and adjust in light of true driving situations, making a criticism circle that meant to upgrade the capacities of the whole armada.

The iterative idea of Tesla's methodology was exemplified with the presentation of the specially crafted Autopilot Equipment 3.0 (HW3) PC. Disclosed in 2019, this equipment overhaul was a vital stage in improving the handling force of Tesla vehicles, empowering further developed brain organizations and preparing for future independent driving elements. The combination of HW3 exhibited Tesla's obligation to equipment development as a critical part of its independent driving system.

In spite of the steps made with Autopilot, Tesla was not happy with halting at semi-independent abilities. The organization held back nothing aggressive objective — accomplishing Full Self-Driving (FSD). The FSD bundle, acquainted as an update with Autopilot, flagged Tesla's obligation to fostering a framework able to do genuine independence, where the vehicle could explore and work without human mediation.

The FSD bundle presented a few new elements, pushing the limits of independent driving capacities. Explore on Autopilot, a huge improvement, permitted Tesla vehicles to naturally drive on assigned interstates, including taking care of path changes and parkway exits. The Bring highlight empowered Tesla proprietors to remotely gather their vehicles inside a restricted reach, exhibiting a brief look at the potential for independent versatility in unambiguous situations.

Tesla's investigation into FSD has been described by consistent refinement and development of abilities. Over-the-air programming refreshes play had an essential impact in this continuous cycle, permitting Tesla to send upgrades and present new functionalities flawlessly.

This approach has given Tesla proprietors a dynamic and developing driving experience, with their vehicles acquiring new capacities over the long run.

The presentation of FSD has likewise blended discussions and conversations inside the car business and administrative bodies. The actual phrasing, with the utilization of "Full Self-Driving," has brought up issues about the assumptions it sets for drivers and people in general.

Starting around my last information update in January 2022, FSD stays a Level 2 mechanization framework, requiring consistent driver oversight, and accomplishing more elevated levels of independence includes tending to complex specialized, administrative, and cultural difficulties.

The General public of Auto Architects (SAE) characterizes levels of driving computerization, going from Level 0 (no robotization) to Even out 5 (full mechanization).

Tesla's Autopilot and FSD are for the most part viewed as at Level 2 mechanization, where the vehicle can deal with specific driving errands however requires consistent human oversight. Progressing to more elevated levels of mechanization, particularly accomplishing full independence, requires tending to specialized obstacles as well as administrative and security contemplations.

Tesla's investigation of independent driving has not been without difficulties and contentions. High-profile episodes including Tesla vehicles working in Autopilot mode, in some cases bringing about mishaps, definitely stand out enough to be noticed to the intricacies of semi-independent frameworks. Examples of drivers abusing or misconstruing the abilities of Autopilot, participating in unsafe ways of behaving, for example, watching motion pictures or dozing while the vehicle is in activity, have raised worries about client schooling and capable utilization of the innovation.

Administrative investigation has been a huge part of Tesla's excursion into independent driving. Various districts and nations have changing guidelines and principles for the organization of independent vehicles. Questions have been raised about the wording utilized by Tesla, for example, the potential turmoil brought about by the expression "Full Self-Driving." Administrative bodies are wrestling with the requirement for clear correspondence, government sanctioned testing methodology, and a system that guarantees the protected sending of independent driving innovations.

The idea of completely independent driving, frequently alluded to as Robotaxi activity, adds one more layer to Tesla's investigation. The vision includes Tesla vehicles working independently as a component of a ride-sharing armada, giving transportation administrations when not being used by their proprietors. While this idea holds guarantee for the fate of metropolitan versatility, it acquaints extra intricacies related with wellbeing, responsibility, and administrative endorsement for sending independent vehicles in a public transportation setting.

One of the highlights that has gathered consideration in Tesla's investigation of independent driving is the ability for Shrewd Bring. This element permits Tesla proprietors to call their vehicles from a parking spot to their area utilizing the Tesla portable application. While Savvy Gather exhibits the potential for expanded comfort and adaptability, it has likewise ignited conversations about the difficulties of guaranteeing safe communications between independent vehicles and walkers or other street clients.

The progressions in independent driving are not restricted to individual vehicles. Tesla has been investigating the idea of an associated armada, where vehicles share data about street conditions, traffic, and possible risks. This vehicle-to-vehicle (V2V) correspondence can improve the aggregate consciousness of the whole armada, making an organization impact where every vehicle benefits from the experiences acquired by others.

Tesla's investigation into independent driving stretches out past the conventional limits of the car business. The interconnectedness of independent vehicles with environmentally friendly power arrangements, energy capacity, and brilliant framework lines up with Tesla's more extensive mission of speeding up the world's change to reasonable energy. The coordination of independent crashing into an all encompassing energy environment adds to the production of a more proficient, safe, and economical transportation worldview.

Starting around my last information update in January 2022, the scene of independent driving is dynamic, with progressing headways and conversations inside the business. Different organizations, including customary automakers and innovation goliaths, are putting vigorously in independent driving innovative work. The opposition in this space is driving development across the auto area, with an emphasis on tending to specialized difficulties, administrative structures, and cultural contemplations.

4.3 Impact on safety and the future of transportation.

Tesla's effect on security and the fate of transportation is significant, originating from its imaginative way to deal with vehicle innovation, high level driver-help frameworks, and its aggressive quest for independent driving abilities. As the auto scene goes through a change towards maintainability and expanded network, Tesla has situated itself as a pioneer, impacting the security principles of the present vehicles as well as forming the direction of transportation in the years to come.

One of the essential mainstays of Tesla's effect on wellbeing lies in its obligation to electric vehicles (EVs). Tesla's choice to zero in solely on electric drive has altered the car business as well as contributed fundamentally to somewhere safe and secure progressions. The intrinsic plan of electric vehicles, with a lower focus of gravity because of the position of weighty battery packs, improves steadiness and decreases the gamble of rollover mishaps.

Tesla's electric vehicles, including the Model S, Model 3, Model X, and Model Y, have reliably exhibited top-level wellbeing execution. The coordination of electric impetus frameworks with state of the art security highlights, like high level driver-help frameworks, has set another norm for vehicle wellbeing. The Model S, for example, accomplished the most elevated wellbeing rating in numerous classes, including NHTSA (Public Roadway Traffic Security Organization) crash tests.

A foundation of Tesla's effect on wellbeing is its Autopilot framework, presented in 2015. Autopilot denoted a huge forward-moving step in the domain of cutting edge driver-help frameworks, presenting highlights like versatile voyage control, programmed path keeping, and programmed path changes. These highlights improve the driving experience as well as add to in general street security by diminishing the probability of crashes and mishaps.

The wellbeing advantages of Autopilot stretch out past the accommodation of mechanized driving undertakings. Tesla's vehicles furnished with Autopilot are outfitted with a set-up of sensors, including cameras, ultrasonic sensors, and radar, giving a thorough perspective on the vehicle's environmental factors. This sensor combination, joined with cutting edge handling abilities, empowers highlights like crash evasion, programmed crisis slowing down, and impediment location, further upgrading the security of Tesla vehicles.

Tesla's obligation to over-the-air (OTA) programming refreshes plays had a urgent impact in persistently further developing the security highlights of its vehicles. The capacity to convey refreshes remotely permits Tesla to address potential wellbeing concerns instantly, present new security elements, and upgrade the exhibition of existing ones. This dynamic and versatile way to deal with vehicle wellbeing is a takeoff from customary models, where security highlights are many times static all through a vehicle's life expectancy.

Nonetheless, Tesla's Autopilot has not been without debate. High-profile episodes including Tesla vehicles working in Autopilot mode have brought up issues about the limits of semi-independent frameworks and the requirement for clear correspondence about client obligations. Cases of drivers abusing or misconstruing the capacities of Autopilot have highlighted the difficulties of guaranteeing dependable utilization of cutting edge driver-help frameworks.

The presentation of the Full Self-Driving (FSD) bundle, expanding upon the groundwork of Autopilot, has additionally extended the security abilities of Tesla vehicles. FSD presents highlights like Explore on Autopilot, permitting programmed driving on assigned parkways, including path changes and thruway exits. While the innovation isn't completely independent starting around my last information update in January 2022, FSD features Tesla's vision for the fate of transportation, where vehicles can explore complex traffic situations and convergences independently.

Tesla's effect on wellbeing goes past the capacities of individual vehicles. The interconnectedness of Tesla's armada, worked with by the persistent growing experience through information assortment, adds to the aggregate wellbeing of all Tesla vehicles out and about. This present reality driving encounters of Tesla vehicles act as significant pieces of information for refining independent driving calculations, recognizing potential wellbeing enhancements, and upgrading the general security of the armada.

The quest for completely independent driving, frequently alluded to as Even out 5 robotization, holds the commitment of a critical decrease in car crashes and fatalities. Human blunder is a main source of street mishaps, and the improvement of frameworks able to do dependably exploring complex traffic situations can possibly moderate the effect of driver-related factors on street wellbeing. In any case, accomplishing full independence includes tending to specialized difficulties as well as administrative, moral, and cultural contemplations.

Tesla's vision for a completely independent future reaches out to the idea of Robotaxis — independently worked Tesla vehicles that can give transportation administrations when not being used by their proprietors. This vision lines up with a more extensive shift towards portability as a help, where clients can get to transportation onrequest without the requirement for vehicle possession. While the acknowledgment of completely independent public transportation faces administrative obstacles and specialized difficulties, the potential security benefits and expanded availability are driving the business towards this groundbreaking vision.

With regards to somewhere safe, Tesla's investigation of independent driving meets with more extensive conversations about the cultural effect of mechanization. Inquiries concerning position dislodging for proficient drivers, changes to transportation framework, and the moral contemplations of programming decision-production into independent frameworks are vital to the bigger discussion about the fate of versatility.

The effect of Tesla's security developments isn't bound to its own prosperity; it has catalyzed a more extensive industry shift towards focusing on wellbeing and propelling vehicle innovation. Customary automakers, once reluctant to completely embrace electric vehicles and independent driving, have sped up their own wellbeing drives and put vigorously in innovative work. The accentuation on wellbeing elements, network, and independence has turned into a cutthroat differentiator in the car business.

Tesla's impact on the fate of transportation stretches out past wellbeing to incorporate the more extensive change towards supportability. The organization's obligation to electric vehicles lines up with worldwide endeavors to lessen ozone depleting substance emanations and battle environmental change. As legislatures and purchasers progressively focus on maintainability, the charge of transportation has turned into a point of convergence for the car business' future.

The outcome of Tesla's electric vehicles has animated a rush of speculation and development in the electric vehicle market. Conventional automakers, perceiving the change in customer inclinations, have sped up their arrangements to jolt their vehicle setups. The expanded reception of electric vehicles adds to bring down outflows as well as cultivates a more supportable and harmless to the ecosystem transportation environment.

The combination of electric vehicles with independent driving advancements further intensifies the potential for manageable transportation. Independent electric vehicles, particularly those working in shared portability armadas, have the ability to advance courses, lessen gridlock, and upgrade by and large transportation proficiency.

This joining lines up with Tesla's more extensive mission of speeding up the world's change to economical energy by tending to the vehicle's power source as well as its functional productivity.

Tesla's effect on the fate of transportation is additionally apparent in the changing elements of metropolitan portability. The idea of shared versatility administrations, empowered via independent driving innovations, holds the possibility to change the manner in which individuals move inside urban areas. The sending of independent ride-sharing armadas could prompt diminished clog, streamlined traffic stream, and further developed admittance to transportation administrations.

Notwithstanding, the acknowledgment of this extraordinary vision faces difficulties connected with administrative systems, framework improvement, and cultural acknowledgment. The reconciliation of independent vehicles into existing transportation frameworks requires insightful preparation and joint effort between partners, including state run administrations, city organizers, and innovation suppliers.

The impact of Tesla's advancements reaches out to the improvement of savvy transportation environments. Tesla's interconnected armada, equipped for sharing data about street conditions, traffic, and expected dangers, represents the capability of vehicle-to-vehicle (V2V) correspondence. This constant trade of information adds to the making of more secure and more productive street organizations, improving the general insight of transportation for clients.

4.4 Challenges and controversies surrounding Autopilot.

Tesla's Autopilot, the high level driver-help framework presented in 2015, has been at the front of auto development, pushing the limits of semi-independent driving. Be that as it may, this innovative jump has not been without its portion of difficulties and discussions. As Autopilot developed and extended its capacities, it turned into a point of convergence for conversations about wellbeing, client figuring out, administrative investigation, and the more extensive ramifications of acquainting semi-independent elements with the mass market.

One of the essential difficulties related with Autopilot lies in client appreciation and mindful use. Tesla's Autopilot framework, notwithstanding its high level capacities, is sorted as Level 2 mechanization as per the General public of Car Architects (SAE). At this level, the vehicle can deal with specific driving undertakings, however it requires steady driver oversight. The test emerges when clients, maybe affected by the expression "Autopilot," confuse the framework as completely independent and misjudge its abilities.

Episodes of drivers abusing Autopilot, participating in dangerous ways of behaving like watching motion pictures, resting, or sitting in the secondary lounge while the vehicle is in activity, stand out. These occurrences feature the urgent requirement for clear correspondence about the constraints of semi-independent frameworks and the significance of guaranteeing that clients completely grasp their job in the driving system.

Tesla's over-the-air programming refreshes, while a vital part of the organization's deftness in sending new highlights and enhancements, likewise add to the test of client understanding. As Autopilot goes through persistent refinement and gains new functionalities, clients should remain informed about the developing capacities and necessities of the framework. This powerful nature of the innovation requires progressing instruction and mindfulness missions to forestall abuse and guarantee safe driving practices.

The administrative scene encompassing independent and semi-independent driving innovations presents one more arrangement of difficulties for Tesla's Autopilot. Various districts and nations have shifting guidelines and principles for the organization of such frameworks, and accomplishing worldwide administrative consistence is an intricate endeavor. Tesla has confronted investigation from administrative specialists, with questions raised about the classification utilized, the framework's wellbeing, and the requirement for more clear correspondence about the capacities and constraints of Autopilot.

The actual wording, especially the utilization of the expression "Autopilot," has been a wellspring of contention. Pundits contend that the term can be deluding, making assumptions that the framework is further developed than its ongoing abilities. This discussion stretches out to the utilization of the expression "Full Self-Driving" (FSD) for Tesla's further developed bundle. Starting around my last information update in January 2022, FSD stays a Level 2 mechanization framework, requiring driver management.

The test of wording isn't just semantic; it has viable ramifications for client conduct and security. Assuming drivers accept that Autopilot suggests full independence, they might be more disposed to separate from the driving errand, prompting potential dangers. Finding some kind of harmony in wording — imparting the capacities precisely while beating overreliance on the innovation down — is a nuanced part of acquainting progressed driver-help frameworks with the market.

Tesla's Autopilot has confronted analysis and doubt, especially in the result of mishaps including vehicles working in Autopilot mode. Mishaps and crashes have prompted examinations by administrative organizations, powering worries about the security of semi-independent driving frameworks. While certain occurrences can be ascribed to abuse or absence of driver consideration, others bring up issues about the framework's capacity to deal with intricate and dynamic driving situations.

The General public of Car Specialists (SAE) characterizes levels of driving mechanization, going from Level 0 (no computerization) to Even out 5 (full robotization). Starting around my last information update in January 2022, Tesla's Autopilot is for the most part viewed as at Level 2 mechanization. Accomplishing more significant levels of robotization includes tending to complex specialized difficulties, administrative investigation, and guaranteeing that the innovation is fit for taking care of many driving situations securely.

One more critical test encompassing Autopilot is the harmony among development and security. Tesla's methodology of conveying highlights in a beta or "Full Self-Driving Sneak peak" state, permitting clients to access and test progressed functionalities that are still being developed, brings up issues about the status of these elements for public streets. The choice to deliver highlights in beta is essential for Tesla's iterative improvement approach, yet it has started banters about the degree of testing, approval, and administrative oversight fundamental for acquainting such elements with a mass shopper market.

Pundits contend that delivering highlights in beta might urge clients to face pointless challenges or take part in ways of behaving that compromise wellbeing. Finding some kind of harmony among development and guaranteeing that highlights are powerful, dependable, and completely tried is quite difficult for organizations creating semi-independent and independent driving advancements.

The job of human variables in semi-independent frameworks adds one more layer of intricacy. The change between computerized driving and human control, known as the handover, is a basic part of Level 2 mechanization. Guaranteeing that drivers can rapidly and really continue control when fundamental is fundamental for keeping up with wellbeing. Be that as it may, the difficulties related with the handover interaction, including driver consideration and response time, remain areas of dynamic innovative work.

Network safety concerns additionally become possibly the most important factor as vehicles become more associated and dependent on programming. The potential for pernicious entertainers to take advantage of weaknesses in the product of associated vehicles represents a gamble to the wellbeing and security of independent and semiindependent frameworks. The requirement for strong network safety measures to safeguard vehicles from hacking and unapproved access is principal as these advances become more pervasive on the streets.

The discussion encompassing Autopilot has started banters inside the car business and among policymakers about the fitting administrative structures for independent and semi-independent driving. Finding some kind of harmony between encouraging development and guaranteeing public wellbeing is a fragile undertaking. Administrative bodies face the test of staying up with the fast progressions in innovation while laying out norms that focus on security and moderate likely dangers.

The difficulties and debates encompassing Autopilot feature the intricacies inborn in the turn of events and arrangement of semi-independent driving advances. Starting around my last information update in January 2022, the scene keeps on developing, with continuous progressions, administrative conversations, and public talk molding the direction of independent and semi-independent driving.

Chapter 5

Resilience Amid Challenges

Tesla's process has been one of strength, set apart by a persistent quest for development, conquering various difficulties, and exploring a scene that frequently appeared to be unconquerable. From its initial days as a juvenile electric vehicle startup to turning into an extraordinary power in the auto and energy enterprises, Tesla's story is a demonstration of the versatility of its visionaries, the flexibility of its methodologies, and the steady obligation to manageability and mechanical progression.

The beginning of Tesla can be followed back to when the auto business was overwhelmed by conventional gas powered motor vehicles. Established in 2003 by Martin Eberhard and Marc Tarpenning, the organization set out with a mission to speed up the world's change to manageable energy. Notwithstanding, the street ahead was laden with difficulties. Distrust about the suitability of electric vehicles, restricted framework for charging, and the monetary dangers related with entering an exceptionally cutthroat industry were critical impediments.

Elon Musk's entrance into Tesla in 2004 denoted a defining moment. Musk, a visionary business person with a history of progress in the tech business, saw the potential for Tesla to disturb the car the norm. Regardless of beginning incredulity, Musk infused genuinely necessary capital into the organization and expected an influential position. His vision reached out past electric vehicles; Musk expected to construct an in an upward direction coordinated energy organization that created electric vehicles as well as upset energy capacity and economical power age.

The car scene introduced an impressive test. Tesla confronted distrust from industry specialists, with questions about the attainability of efficiently manufacturing electric vehicles and worries about the restricted scope of early electric vehicle models. The organization's most memorable item, the Tesla Roadster, was an elite presentation sports vehicle that displayed the capability of electric powertrains yet confronted difficulties regarding reasonableness and openness.

Determined by the underlying obstacles, Tesla drove forward. The divulging of the Model S in 2012 denoted a crucial second. This all-electric car not just exhibited

Tesla's obligation to making electric vehicles with mass-market claim yet additionally displayed the organization's ability in plan, innovation, and execution. The Model S got broad praise, testing assumptions about electric vehicles and laying out Tesla as a serious competitor in the car business.

Nonetheless, Tesla's versatility was tried on different fronts. The excursion to large scale manufacturing was laden with assembling difficulties, store network intricacies, and monetary tensions. The organization confronted incredulity from customary automakers and monetary investigators who questioned Tesla's capacity to scale creation and make money. Musk's aggressive objectives, including the Gigafactory — an enormous office for battery creation — confronted distrust and examination.

Tesla's entrance into the mass market with the more reasonable Model 3 introduced both an open door and a test. The organization expected to make electric vehicles open to a more extensive crowd, however accomplishing this objective required tending to assembling versatility, meeting creation targets, and defeating strategic obstacles. The creation increase for the Model 3 was defaced by delays, creation bottlenecks, and expanded investigation from financial backers and the media.

The monetary difficulties mounted, prompting hypothesis about Tesla's drawn out feasibility. Incredulity arrived at its top as the organization confronted inquiries concerning its capacity to meet obligation commitments, accomplish benefit, and support its aggressive development plans. The tenacious examination from short-merchants and doubters turned into a central quality of Tesla's excursion, establishing a climate where each mishap was amplified.

Regardless of the headwinds, Tesla showed astounding flexibility. The organization faced the hardship as well as arisen more grounded. The fruitful creation increase of the Model 3, accomplishing mass-market moderateness, and outperforming creation targets exhibited Tesla's capacity to gain from difficulties, adjust its procedures, and execute on its vision. The Gigafactory, once saw with wariness, turned into a foundation of Tesla's assembling capacities and made light of an essential job in driving the expense of batteries.

Development has been a steady subject in Tesla's excursion, and the organization's capacity to defeat difficulties through mechanical headways has been a key differentiator. The improvement of Autopilot, Tesla's high level driver-help framework, addressed a jump forward in auto innovation. Nonetheless, Autopilot likewise brought difficulties, including administrative examination, wellbeing concerns, and discussions about client getting it and capable use.

The strength of Tesla was apparent in its reaction to these difficulties. The organization iteratively further developed Autopilot through over-the-air programming refreshes, refining its capacities, tending to somewhere safe worries, and presenting new highlights. The obligation to ceaseless improvement displayed Tesla's flexibility and its ability to explore the unique scene of independent driving innovation.

The discussions encompassing Autopilot, including high-profile occurrences and administrative examination, featured the intricacies of acquainting semi-independent elements with the mass market. Tesla confronted difficulties in overseeing client assumptions, tending to somewhere safe and secure worries, and guaranteeing dependable utilization of the innovation. The requirement for clear correspondence, training, and cooperation with administrative bodies became critical components of Tesla's procedure to beat these difficulties.

Tesla's versatility stretches out past the car area into the energy business. The organization's introduction to energy capacity with items like the Powerwall and Powerpack, and its drive into sunlight based energy with the procurement of SolarCity, exhibited a more extensive vision for a maintainable energy biological system. Be that as it may, challenges emerged in coordinating SolarCity, monetary tensions built, and cynics scrutinized the essential reasoning behind the obtaining.

Yet again tesla adjusted to the difficulties. The improvement of the Powerwall, a home battery framework, tended to energy capacity needs and situated Tesla as a central member in the change to environmentally friendly power. The revealing of the sun oriented rooftop, coordinating sun powered chargers into roofing materials, exhibited Tesla's obligation to feel and usefulness in sun based energy arrangements. The essential turn from sun powered renting to coordinate deals additionally highlighted the organization's capacity to adjust its plan of action because of market elements.

The difficulties related with scaling energy stockpiling arrangements and exploring administrative scenes for sunlight based establishments required a blend of mechanical development, vital organizations, and commitment with policymakers. Tesla's versatility was clear in its capacity to explore these intricacies, gain from difficulties, and position itself as a forerunner in the quickly developing sustainable power area.

The worldwide change toward electric vehicles and economical energy arrangements has additionally prompted difficulties connected with store network elements. The interest for electric vehicles and energy stockpiling arrangements has stressed worldwide inventory chains for basic parts like batteries and semiconductor chips. The business wide chip lack, exacerbated by the Coronavirus pandemic, presented moves for Tesla and its capacity to meet creation targets.

Yet again accordingly, Tesla showed flexibility through essential independent direction and inventory network enhancement. The organization enhanced its hotspots for basic parts, investigated elective production network systems, and utilized its in-house fabricating abilities to relieve the effect of outside disturbances. The capacity to adjust to unexpected difficulties and proactively address production network weaknesses featured Tesla's dexterity and strength even with dynamic economic situations.

Ecological and international factors additionally introduced difficulties for Tesla. The reliance on intriguing earth metals and other natural substances expected for electric vehicle batteries raised worries about the ecological effect of asset extraction. Furthermore, international pressures and exchange elements impacted the accessibility and estimating of basic materials. Tesla's obligation to manageability confronted examination, and the organization explored difficulties related with mindful obtaining and natural effect.

As Tesla extended its worldwide impression, it experienced administrative difficulties in various locales. Changing principles for vehicle security, discharges, and independent driving presented intricacies for an organization with a worldwide client base. Exploring assorted administrative scenes required key commitment with policymakers, adherence to nearby guidelines, and continuous joint effort with administrative specialists.

5.1 Navigating Business Challenges

Tesla, a pioneer in the auto and energy areas, has explored a mind boggling scene overflowing with difficulties, exhibiting versatility, flexibility, and an unflinching obligation to its central goal. From its beginning in 2003 to its ongoing status as an extraordinary power in the worldwide market, Tesla's process has been characterized by defeating obstacles, embracing development, and rethinking industry norms.

One of the early difficulties looked by Tesla was the wariness encompassing the feasibility of electric vehicles (EVs). In the mid 2000s, the car business was settled in the strength of gas powered motor vehicles. Tesla's organizers, Martin Eberhard and Marc Tarpenning, imagined a future where electric vehicles could be both down to earth and attractive. In any case, getting through the wariness required mechanical development as well as a change in purchaser discernments.

Enter Elon Musk, who joined Tesla in 2004, infusing truly necessary capital and vision into the organization. Musk, known for his part in PayPal and SpaceX, carried a new point of view to the electric vehicle market. His vision stretched out past making electric vehicles; he expected to disturb the whole auto industry and speed up the change to manageable energy. Musk's administration denoted a defining moment, changing Tesla from an aggressive startup into an amazing powerhouse in the auto and energy areas.

Tesla's introduction to the auto market was not without monetary dangers. The turn of events and creation of electric vehicles required significant capital, and doubters addressed whether Tesla could prevail in an industry known for its high boundaries to passage. Musk's aggressive objectives, like efficiently manufacturing reasonable electric vehicles, fabricating the Gigafactory for battery creation, and making an in an upward direction coordinated energy organization, confronted examination from financial backers and industry specialists the same.

The difficulties increased with the development of Tesla's most memorable vehicle, the Roadster. While the Roadster exhibited the capability of electric impetus in an elite execution sports vehicle, it confronted difficulties connected with moderateness and openness. Tesla's turn to the mass market was highlighted by the presentation of the Model S in 2012, an extravagance car that consolidated exhibition with a lengthy electric reach. The Model S got basic praise, however challenges continued, including fabricating adaptability and monetary tensions.

The mass-market desires turned out to be considerably more articulated with the presentation of the Model 3. Tesla planned to make electric vehicles open to a more extensive crowd, however the creation increase presented huge difficulties. Producing bottlenecks, delays, and expanded examination from financial backers and the media portrayed this period. The outcome of the Model 3, both as far as creation numbers and buyer reception, showed Tesla's capacity to gain from difficulties, adjust techniques, and accomplish mass-market moderateness.

The monetary difficulties were joined by suspicion from short-merchants and pundits who scrutinized Tesla's drawn out practicality. Musk's aggressive objectives, including the colonization of Mars through SpaceX, prompted questions about the plausibility of at the same time dealing with various noteworthy endeavors. The consistent examination established a climate where each mishap or defer confronted amplification, yet Tesla's capacity to get capital, accomplish productivity, and out-perform creation targets exhibited its strength.

Tesla's deftness was further apparent in its reaction to the business wide chip lack, exacerbated by the Coronavirus pandemic. The lack presented difficulties to meeting creation targets, however Tesla differentiated its hotspots for basic parts, investigated elective store network systems, and utilized its in-house fabricating abilities. This pro-active methodology exhibited Tesla's capacity to explore unanticipated difficulties and improve its store network notwithstanding powerful economic situations.

Natural and international elements added layers of intricacy. The worldwide push towards manageability expanded the interest for electric vehicles, yet worries about the ecological effect of asset extraction for EV batteries arose. Tesla confronted diffi-culties connected with capable obtaining and natural effect, exploring a scene where ESG (Ecological, Social, and Administration) contemplations became essential to corporate system.

The organization's worldwide extension brought administrative difficulties as shift-ing norms for vehicle security, outflows, and independent driving existed in various locales. Tesla needed to adjust its vehicles to consent to different guidelines and draw in with policymakers to guarantee consistence. Exploring these administrative scenes expected vital reasoning and a continuous obligation to satisfying worldwide guidelines.

Tesla's strength additionally radiated through notwithstanding debates encom-passing Autopilot, its high level driver-help framework. High-profile episodes and administrative examination uplifted the intricacies of acquainting semi-independent elements with the mass market. Tesla tended to somewhere safe worries through over-the-air programming refreshes, refined Autopilot's abilities, and presented new elements. The organization's iterative methodology exhibited a capacity to gain from mishaps and improve security highlights in light of advancing difficulties.

The obtaining of SolarCity, a sun oriented energy organization, in 2016 was met with suspicion and monetary examination. Pundits scrutinized the essential reasoning behind the securing, and monetary difficulties mounted as Tesla tried to incorporate SolarCity into its more extensive vision of a feasible energy biological system. Be that as it may, Tesla adjusted its plan of action, displaying versatility by turning from sunlight based renting to coordinate deals and reinforcing its situation in the sustainable power area.

The interconnected idea of Tesla's organizations — electric vehicles, energy capacity, and sunlight based energy — implied that difficulties in a single area could influence others. Adjusting to the powerful scene of every industry expected an all encompassing methodology and a capacity to offset development with monetary maintainability. Tesla's outcome in turning into a central part in both the car and energy areas highlighted its ability to explore different difficulties.

Tesla's vision extended past individual items to incorporate a coordinated energy biological system. The advancement of energy stockpiling arrangements like the Powerwall and Powerpack tended to the requirement for productive energy stockpiling at various scales. Tesla situated itself as an innovator in the change to sustainable power, offering electric vehicles as well as answers for reasonable power age and capacity.

Exploring the energy scene additionally involved addressing difficulties connected with matrix coordination, administrative structures, and customer reception. Tesla's capacity to adjust its energy items to worldwide patterns towards sustainable power, combined with mechanical development, exhibited its flexibility in forming the eventual fate of energy.

The worldwide component of Tesla's tasks added international contemplations. Exchange elements, tax influences, and worldwide political movements impacted Tesla's capacity to work in various locales. The need to get a steady store network, explore exchange strains, and adjust to changing international scenes required key reasoning and versatility.

5.2 Examination of production hurdles and regulatory obstacles.

The excursion of Tesla, from an aggressive startup to a groundbreaking power in the auto and energy enterprises, has been set apart by an assessment of creation obstacles and administrative impediments. These difficulties play had a crucial impact in forming Tesla's methodologies, impacting its mechanical developments, and testing its versatility. From assembling versatility to administrative scenes, Tesla's capacity to explore these intricacies has been a characterizing part of its development.

One of the early creation obstacles Tesla confronted was the suspicion encompassing the large scale manufacturing of electric vehicles (EVs). The car business, settled in the worldview of gas powered motor vehicles, saw electric vehicles with wariness. The overarching thought was that electric vehicles were illogical, needed range, and confronted huge difficulties regarding large scale manufacturing. Conquering this discernment and showing the reasonability of efficiently manufacturing electric vehicles turned into a crucial test for Tesla.

The development of Tesla's most memorable vehicle, the Roadster, was a demonstration of the organization's obligation to defeating these obstacles. The Roadster exhibited the capability of electric impetus in a superior execution sports vehicle yet confronted difficulties connected with reasonableness and openness. The creation cycle of the Roadster gave important bits of knowledge into the intricacies of assembling electric vehicles at scale.

As Tesla extended its item setup with the presentation of the Model S, an extravagance car, and later the Model 3 for mass-market moderateness, the creation challenges heightened. Accomplishing versatility in assembling turned into a basic concentration. The organization expected to create electric vehicles not in restricted amounts but rather on a scale that could rival customary automakers. This required tending to bottlenecks, improving creation lines, and smoothing out production network processes.

The aggressive objectives set by Elon Musk, Tesla's Chief, added one more layer of intricacy to creation challenges. The presentation of the Gigafactory — a gigantic office committed to battery creation — was an essential move to address difficulties connected with the stock and cost of batteries. Be that as it may, the development and operationalization of such an office brought its own arrangement of obstacles, including monetary tensions and strategic intricacies.

Creation challenges were additionally exemplified during the rollout of the Model 3, Tesla's mass-market electric vehicle. The interest for the Model 3 was exceptional, yet meeting creation targets turned into a Colossal undertaking. The alleged "creation damnation" period was set apart by deferrals, bottlenecks, and expanded investigation from financial backers and the media. Tesla's capacity to defeat these difficulties and increase creation displayed its versatility and assurance to accomplish mass-market moderateness.

The imaginative way to deal with creation reached out to Tesla's utilization of over-the-air (OTA) programming refreshes. Not at all like conventional automakers, Tesla could remotely send updates to its vehicles, resolving issues, further developing execution, and adding new highlights. This unique way to deal with programming sending turned into a vital component in Tesla's procedure for nonstop improvement and permitted the organization to address creation challenges quickly and effectively.

In any case, administrative snags have been entwined with Tesla's creation challenges. The auto business is dependent upon a complicated trap of guidelines, changing from one district to another. Wellbeing principles, emanations necessities, and independent driving guidelines are among the elements that request consistence and impact how vehicles are planned and created.

One eminent model is the administrative investigation encompassing Tesla's Autopilot, a high level driver-help framework. As Tesla sought after development in independent driving innovation, it experienced administrative obstacles connected with security guidelines and the sending of semi-independent elements. Accomplishing administrative endorsement and exploring the fragile harmony among development and wellbeing turned into a multi-layered challenge for Tesla.

The phrasing used to depict Tesla's independent driving highlights, for example, "Autopilot" and "Full Self-Driving" (FSD), confronted analysis for possibly deceptive buyers about the capacities of the innovation. Administrative bodies raised worries about the requirement for more clear correspondence and the expected gamble of clients misjudging the independence of their vehicles. This examination featured the convergence of mechanical development and administrative consistence, outlining the requirement for arrangement between industry headways and administrative systems.

The worldwide development of Tesla's activities presented extra layers of administrative intricacy. Fluctuating principles for vehicle wellbeing, emanations, and independent driving in various areas expected Tesla to adjust its vehicles to conform to different guidelines. Exploring these administrative scenes requested vital reasoning, commitment with policymakers, and continuous endeavors to guarantee Tesla's consistence with worldwide principles.

The obtaining of SolarCity, a sun based energy organization, added administrative difficulties to Tesla's portfolio. The coordination of SolarCity into Tesla's vision of a feasible energy biological system confronted monetary investigation and administrative obstacles. Pundits scrutinized the essential reasoning behind the securing, and administrative bodies examined the monetary ramifications for Tesla. The need to adjust energy items to developing administrative scenes turned into a vital part of Tesla's strength even with difficulties.

Natural guidelines and discharges principles likewise affected Tesla's creation procedures. As state run administrations overall looked to decrease fossil fuel byproducts and battle environmental change, the auto business confronted expanding strain to progress to electric vehicles. Tesla, situated as a forerunner in electric versatility, needed to adjust its creation processes with these developing natural contemplations. The ecological effect of asset extraction for EV batteries and dependable obtaining of materials became vital parts of Tesla's creation system.

The worldwide push towards supportability, combined with expanding attention to environmental change, raised the significance of ecological contemplations for organizations. Tesla's obligation to maintainability confronted examination, and the organization explored difficulties related with capable obtaining, ecological effect appraisals, and meeting advancing ESG (Natural, Social, and Administration) norms.

International contemplations added one more layer of intricacy to Tesla's creation challenges. Exchange elements, levy influences, and worldwide political movements impacted Tesla's capacity to work in various locales. The need to get a steady store network, explore exchange pressures, and adjust to changing international scenes required vital reasoning and flexibility on Tesla's part.

5.3 How Tesla faced challenges head-on and evolved.

Tesla's excursion from an aggressive electric vehicle startup to a worldwide forerunner in economical transportation and energy arrangements has been set apart by a wonderful capacity to deal with difficulties directly and develop because of a quickly evolving scene. From assembling obstacles to administrative examination and market wariness, Tesla's flexibility and versatility have been instrumental in forming its direction and hardening its situation as a groundbreaking power in the auto and energy ventures.

One of the early difficulties Tesla confronted was the distrust encompassing the large scale manufacturing of electric vehicles (EVs). As the car business stuck to conventional gas powered motors, Tesla's organizers, Martin Eberhard and Marc Tarpenning, imagined a future where electric vehicles could be both commonsense and attractive. This vision, nonetheless, was met with incredulity about the plausibility of efficiently manufacturing electric vehicles at a scale that could rival conventional automakers.

The section of Elon Musk in 2004 denoted a defining moment for Tesla. Musk, known for his part in PayPal and SpaceX, carried truly necessary money to the organization as well as a striking vision that reached out past electric vehicles. Musk expected to disturb the whole car industry, speed up the world's change to feasible energy, and fabricate an in an upward direction coordinated energy organization. Tesla's change from a specialty electric vehicle maker to a diverse energy and transportation organization started to come to fruition under Musk's initiative.

The creation obstacles were exacerbated by monetary difficulties. Creating and fabricating electric vehicles required significant capital, and Tesla confronted wariness about its capacity to make money and accomplish long haul reasonability. Musk's aggressive objectives, including efficiently manufacturing reasonable electric vehicles and building the Gigafactory for battery creation, confronted examination from financial backers and industry specialists who questioned Tesla's ability to scale creation and contend in a profoundly cutthroat market.

Tesla's reaction to these difficulties was not only responsive; it was proactive and imaginative. Musk's emphasis on vertical combination, exemplified by the Gigafactory, intended to address creation challenges as well as the basic issue of battery supply. By getting battery creation house, Tesla tried to get a steady inventory network, lessen expenses, and scale up creation to fulfill the developing need for electric vehicles.

The development of Tesla's most memorable vehicle, the Roadster, gave early experiences into the difficulties related with assembling electric vehicles. The Roadster, a superior exhibition sports vehicle, displayed the capability of electric impetus yet confronted obstacles connected with moderateness and openness. In any case, Tesla gained important examples from this experience, laying the foundation for future models that would focus on a more extensive market.

As Tesla extended its item setup with models like the Model S, an extravagance car, and later the Model 3 for mass-market reasonableness, the organization faced the requirement for assembling versatility. Accomplishing large scale manufacturing of electric vehicles turned into a focal concentration, and Tesla's capacity to explore these difficulties became inseparable from its ability for development and versatility.

The presentation of the Model 3, Tesla's mass-market electric vehicle, introduced an essential second and a huge trial of the organization's creation capacities. The interest for the Model 3 was uncommon, however meeting creation targets turned into a Considerable undertaking. The purported "creation damnation" period was set apart by deferrals, bottlenecks, and expanded examination from financial backers and the media.

As opposed to capitulating to the tension, Tesla answered with spryness and assurance. The organization executed iterative enhancements, streamlined creation lines, and addressed bottlenecks to increase creation. The utilization of over-the-air (OTA) programming refreshes permitted Tesla to remotely convey refreshes, upgrading execution, resolving issues, and adding new elements. This powerful way to deal with programming sending turned into a vital component in Tesla's technique for nonstop improvement and permitted the organization to explore creation challenges quickly and proficiently.

Tesla's capacity to develop innovatively and defeat creation obstacles was not restricted to its vehicles. The Gigafactory, an enormous office for battery creation, was an essential move that exhibited Tesla's ground breaking approach.

The Gigafactory not just addressed difficulties connected with the stock and cost of batteries yet additionally situated Tesla as a key part in energy capacity, a fundamental part of the organization's vision for a manageable energy biological system.

Be that as it may, the difficulties for Tesla reached out past the creation floor. Administrative examination, an inborn part of the auto business, turned into a critical consider Tesla's development. Wellbeing principles, outflows necessities, and independent driving guidelines requested consistence and impacted how Tesla's vehicles were planned, created, and worked.

One remarkable model is the administrative investigation encompassing Tesla's Autopilot, a high level driver-help framework. As Tesla sought after development in independent driving innovation, it experienced administrative obstacles connected with security norms and the arrangement of semi-independent elements. The need to accomplish administrative endorsement and explore the fragile harmony among development and security turned into a multi-layered challenge for Tesla.

The wording used to depict Tesla's independent driving highlights, for example, "Autopilot" and "Full Self-Driving" (FSD), confronted analysis for possibly deceptive purchasers about the abilities of the innovation. Administrative bodies raised worries about the requirement for more clear correspondence and the likely gamble of clients misjudging the independence of their vehicles. This examination featured the convergence of mechanical development and administrative consistence, outlining the requirement for arrangement between industry progressions and administrative structures.

Tesla's reaction to administrative difficulties was portrayed by coordinated effort, persistent improvement, and a promise to somewhere safe. The organization worked intimately with administrative bodies, carried out wellbeing highlights through programming refreshes, and participated in continuous correspondence to guarantee that its independent driving advances lined up with developing administrative assumptions.

The worldwide development of Tesla's tasks presented extra layers of administrative intricacy. Fluctuating norms for vehicle security, emanations, and independent driving in various locales expected Tesla to adjust its vehicles to follow different guidelines. Exploring these administrative scenes requested key reasoning, commitment with policymakers, and continuous endeavors to guarantee Tesla's consistency with worldwide guidelines.

The procurement of SolarCity, a sunlight based energy organization, added one more aspect to Tesla's administrative difficulties. The mix of SolarCity into Tesla's vision of a reasonable energy biological system confronted monetary investigation and administrative obstacles. Pundits scrutinized the essential reasoning behind the procurement, and administrative bodies investigated the monetary ramifications for Tesla. The need to adjust energy items to developing administrative scenes turned into a vital part of Tesla's flexibility notwithstanding challenges.

Natural guidelines and outflows principles likewise impacted Tesla's creation procedures. As state run administrations overall tried to diminish fossil fuel byproducts and battle environmental change, the auto business confronted expanding strain to progress to electric vehicles. Tesla, situated as a forerunner in electric versatility, needed to adjust its creation processes with these developing natural contemplations. The natural effect of asset extraction for EV batteries and mindful obtaining of materials became vital parts of Tesla's creation technique.

The worldwide push towards maintainability, combined with expanding consciousness of environmental change, raised the significance of natural contemplations for organizations. Tesla's obligation to supportability confronted investigation, and the organization explored difficulties related with dependable obtaining, ecological effect evaluations, and meeting developing ESG (Natural, Social, and Administration) norms.

International contemplations added one more layer of intricacy to Tesla's creation challenges. Exchange elements, levy influences, and worldwide political movements impacted Tesla's capacity to work in various districts. The need to get a steady production network, explore exchange pressures, and adjust to changing international scenes required vital reasoning and flexibility on Tesla's part.

5.4 The resilience that shaped Tesla's corporate culture.

Tesla's corporate excursion has been portrayed by mechanical development and market disturbance as well as by a particular corporate culture set apart by flexibility. From its initial days as a startup rocking the boat of the auto business to its flow position as a worldwide forerunner in electric vehicles and supportable energy arrangements, Tesla's flexibility has been a main impetus forming its hierarchical DNA.

At the center of Tesla's flexibility is its unflinching obligation to an intense and extraordinary mission: to speed up the world's change to supportable energy. This mission, set by the organization's pioneers and embraced by Chief Elon Musk, has filled in as a directing light, giving a feeling of motivation that rises above the difficulties experienced en route. The obligation to supportability and the bold objective of reshaping the energy scene have become necessary components of Tesla's corporate personality.

One of the fundamental parts of Tesla's corporate culture is its ability to challenge regular standards. In the mid 2000s, the car business was settled in the strength of gas powered motor vehicles, with electric vehicles considered unreasonable and unappealing to the mass market. Tesla, be that as it may, thought about testing this insight. The organization's originators, Martin Eberhard and Marc Tarpenning, imagined electric vehicles not as specialty items but rather as a suitable and convincing option in contrast to conventional vehicles.

Elon Musk's entrance into Tesla in 2004 denoted a crucial second in the organization's direction. Musk, known for his job in PayPal and SpaceX, brought a visionary standpoint that reached out past electric vehicles.

Musk's initiative style, portrayed by intensity and a readiness to take on colossal difficulties, turned into a characterizing component of Tesla's corporate culture. Musk's methodology reflected the ethos of Silicon Valley, where interruption and advancement are commended, and moonshot desires are supported as well as anticipated.

The capacity to explore monetary moves has been one more demonstration of Tesla's flexibility. The turn of events and creation of electric vehicles required significant capital, and Tesla confronted wariness about its capacity to make money. Musk's aggressive objectives, for example, efficiently manufacturing reasonable electric vehicles and building the Gigafactory for battery creation, confronted examination from financial backers and industry specialists who questioned Tesla's ability to scale creation and contend in an exceptionally cutthroat market.

Tesla's reaction to monetary difficulties exhibited flexibility and a refusal to stick to the state of affairs. Rather than capitulating to the strain of ordinary monetary insight, Tesla looked to reclassify the guidelines of the game. Musk's choice to make Tesla a public organization in 2010 was an essential move that expected to get the fundamental capital for the organization's aggressive objectives. This choice tested customary funding strategies as well as denoted Tesla's obligation to straightforwardness and responsibility, key components of its corporate culture.

The creation obstacles looked by Tesla were met with an assurance to enhance and emphasize. The creation of the Roadster, Tesla's most memorable vehicle, gave significant bits of knowledge into the difficulties related with assembling electric vehicles. While the Roadster exhibited the capability of electric drive in a superior execution sports vehicle, it likewise confronted obstacles connected with reasonableness and openness. In any case, Tesla utilized these difficulties as learning potential open doors, refining its way to deal with plan, creation, and versatility.

The ensuing presentation of the Model S in 2012 denoted a vital second for Tesla. This all-electric car not just shown Tesla's obligation to making electric vehicles with mass-market bid yet in addition displayed the organization's ability in plan, innovation, and execution. The Model S got far and wide recognition, testing assumptions about electric vehicles and laying out Tesla as a serious competitor in the car business.

The extension of Tesla's item arrangement, including the more reasonable Model 3, further highlighted the organization's strength. The difficulties of large scale manufacturing, fabricating versatility, and accomplishing moderateness were met with a guarantee to persistent improvement. Tesla's versatility became clear in its reaction to the purported "creation damnation" period during the rollout of the Model 3. The organization carried out iterative upgrades, improved creation lines, and addressed bottlenecks to satisfy the exceptional need for its mass-market electric car.

Tesla's corporate culture embraces a quick emphasis cycle, a trademark more similar to innovation organizations than conventional automakers. The utilization of over-the-air (OTA) programming refreshes is a perfect representation of this methodology. Dissimilar to conventional automakers, Tesla can remotely send updates to its vehicles, resolving issues, further developing execution, and adding new highlights. This powerful way to deal with programming organization features Tesla's innovative ability as well as epitomizes a culture of consistent improvement and versatility.

At the core of Tesla's corporate culture is a readiness to embrace hazard and vulnerability. Musk's aggressive objectives, including the colonization of Mars through SpaceX, prompted questions about the plausibility of all the while dealing with different momentous endeavors. The consistent investigation from short-venders and doubters established a climate where each misfortune or postpone confronted amplification. However, Tesla's readiness to take on aggressive undertakings, combined with a comprehension of the innate dangers, has been a main impetus behind its capacity to develop and disturb.

The debates encompassing Autopilot, Tesla's high level driver-help framework, featured the intricacies of acquainting semi-independent elements with the mass market. Tesla confronted difficulties in overseeing client assumptions, tending to somewhere safe worries, and guaranteeing mindful utilization of the innovation. The requirement for clear correspondence, instruction, and coordinated effort with administrative bodies became urgent components of Tesla's system to conquer these difficulties.

The securing of SolarCity in 2016 was met with doubt and monetary examination. Pundits scrutinized the essential reasoning behind the securing, and monetary difficulties mounted as Tesla looked to incorporate SolarCity into its more extensive vision of a manageable energy environment. Notwithstanding, Tesla adjusted its plan of action, displaying versatility by turning from sun powered renting to coordinate deals and supporting its situation in the sustainable power area.

Tesla's flexibility stretches out past the auto area into the energy business. The organization's introduction to energy capacity with items like the Powerwall and Powerpack, and its drive into sun oriented energy with the obtaining of SolarCity, displayed a more extensive vision for a supportable energy biological system. In any case, challenges emerged in coordinating SolarCity, monetary tensions built, and doubters scrutinized the essential reasoning behind the securing.

Yet again tesla adjusted to the difficulties. The improvement of the Powerwall, a home battery framework, tended to energy capacity needs and situated Tesla as a central participant in the progress to environmentally friendly power. The disclosing of the sun powered rooftop, coordinating sunlight based chargers into roofing materials, exhibited Tesla's obligation to style and usefulness in sun oriented energy arrangements.

Chapter 6

Musk's Leadership Odyssey

Elon Musk's initiative at Tesla addresses a convincing and turbulent odyssey, set apart by nervy objectives, weighty development, monetary difficulties, and a steady quest for groundbreaking change. As the fellow benefactor and Chief of Tesla, Musk has been the main thrust behind the organization's development from a beginning electric vehicle startup to a worldwide forerunner in manageable transportation and energy arrangements. His initiative style, portrayed by an exceptional mix of vision, strength, and an eagerness to take on apparently unconquerable difficulties, has made a permanent imprint on both Tesla and the more extensive business scene.

Musk's entrance into Tesla in 2004 was an extraordinary second for the organization. Around then, Tesla was an aggressive startup with a dream to upset the car business by making electric vehicles both down to earth and attractive. The organizers, Martin Eberhard and Marc Tarpenning, had laid the preparation, yet the organization confronted monetary difficulties and suspicion from the conventional auto foundation.

Musk, definitely known for his prosperity with PayPal and SpaceX, brought capital as well as a visionary standpoint that stretched out past electric vehicles. All along, Musk enunciated a mission for Tesla that went past building electric vehicles. He imagined a future where supportable energy arrangements wouldn't just power vehicles yet additionally structure a far reaching environment, tending to the world's reliance on petroleum derivatives.

Under Musk's initiative, Tesla's statement of purpose advanced to mirror this more extensive vision: to speed up the world's progress to manageable energy. This mission turned into the north star directing Tesla's undertakings, affecting its item improvement, business techniques, and, surprisingly, Musk's own interests in practical energy projects.

Musk's initiative at Tesla is recognized by an eagerness to lay out and seek after aggressive objectives that challenge regular industry standards. One of his initial goals was to demonstrate that electric vehicles could be something other than ecologically cognizant; they could be elite execution, alluring, and, significantly, reasonable. The development of the Tesla Roadster, the organization's most memorable vehicle, set the vibe for this daring aspiration.

The Roadster, a superior exhibition electric games vehicle, displayed the capability of electric impetus however confronted difficulties connected with reasonableness and openness. Musk's initiative during this period showed a pledge to conquering obstacles and refining Tesla's methodology. The Roadster filled in as a venturing stone, demonstrating that electric vehicles could contend in the superior execution auto portion, while establishing the groundwork for additional open models from now on.

Musk's administration became the overwhelming focus with the presentation of the Model S in 2012. This all-electric extravagance car not just tested the view of electric vehicles as specialty items yet in addition showed the way that they could outflank conventional gas powered motor vehicles concerning velocity, speed increase, and plan. The Model S got boundless praise, winning various honors and cementing Tesla's situation as a serious player in the auto business.

Nonetheless, Musk's initiative was not without its portion of difficulties. Tesla's venture into the mass market with the Model 3 was met with suspicion and investigation. Accomplishing large scale manufacturing at scale turned into an imposing undertaking, and Tesla confronted what Musk broadly alluded to as "creation damnation." This period was set apart by delays, creation bottlenecks, and expanded strain from financial backers and the media.

Musk's reaction to these difficulties displayed an initiative style described by flexibility and an assurance to conquer hindrances. The execution of iterative enhancements, streamlining of creation lines, and tending to bottlenecks were characteristic of Musk's active way to deal with critical thinking. The capacity to explore these difficulties and satisfy the phenomenal need for the Model 3 featured Musk's strength and ability to lead Tesla through tempestuous times.

A characterizing component of Musk's initiative at Tesla is his obligation to mechanical development. Musk's vision reaches out past electric vehicles to incorporate an extensive practical energy environment. The improvement of the Gigafactory, a monstrous office committed to battery creation, was an essential move pointed toward addressing difficulties connected with the stockpile and cost of batteries.

The Gigafactory not just gotten a steady production network for Tesla yet additionally situated the organization as a central part in energy capacity, a basic part of the change to sustainable power. Musk's emphasis on vertical reconciliation, from assembling batteries to creating electric vehicles, mirrored an all encompassing way to deal with manageability and flexibility notwithstanding a consistently developing energy scene.

Tesla's introduction to independent driving innovation is one more demonstration of Musk's obligation to development. The presentation of Autopilot, a high level driver-help framework, and the aggressive objective of accomplishing Full Self-Driving

(FSD) ability displayed Musk's eagerness to push innovative limits. In any case, this introduction to independence was not without discussion and administrative examination, bringing up issues about security and the status of the innovation for mass organization.

Musk's initiative style is described by a penchant for risk-taking and a craving for handling complex difficulties. The disputable obtaining of SolarCity in 2016 exemplified this methodology. Musk, upholding for a consistent incorporation of sun powered energy arrangements with Tesla's electric vehicles and energy stockpiling items, confronted doubt and monetary examination. Pundits scrutinized the essential reasoning behind the procurement, and the monetary tensions built.

In light of these difficulties, Musk displayed his capacity to adjust and turn. The mix of SolarCity into Tesla's more extensive vision for a practical energy biological system included key movements, including a change from sunlight based renting to coordinate deals. This variation showed Musk's strength despite monetary and vital difficulties, supporting Tesla's situation in the environmentally friendly power area.

Musk's initiative reaches out past the limits of Tesla, enveloping endeavors like SpaceX and The Exhausting Organization. The venturesome objective of colonizing Mars and the improvement of the Hyperloop transportation idea represent Musk's craving for groundbreaking change on a worldwide scale. These endeavors, while particular from Tesla, mirror Musk's overall vision for reshaping enterprises and tending to a portion of humankind's most squeezing difficulties.

Nonetheless, Musk's authority style isn't without contention. His straightforward and some of the time capricious conduct via virtual entertainment has drawn both appreciation and analysis. Musk's utilization of Twitter, specifically, has prompted market unpredictability, lawful difficulties, and administrative investigation. The public persona of Musk, frequently depicted through his tweets and connections, adds a layer of intricacy to his initiative story.

The contentions encompassing Musk, from his public assertions to fights in court and conflicts with administrative specialists, highlight the difficulties of driving an organization as powerful and compelling as Tesla. The double job of Musk as both Chief and a well known individual with a huge virtual entertainment presence adds a layer of intricacy to Tesla's corporate administration and brings up issues about the convergence of individual and corporate initiative.

Notwithstanding the contentions, Musk's administration has been instrumental in moving Tesla to the front of the auto and energy businesses. His capacity to explain a convincing vision, put forth aggressive objectives, and explore through difficulties has become inseparable from Tesla's corporate culture.

Musk's strength, versatility, and ability to take on tremendous difficulties have made a permanent imprint on Tesla's direction and its job in forming the eventual fate of transportation and energy.

6.1 Leadership Style of Elon Musk

Elon Musk, the cryptic and visionary business person, has arisen as a focal figure in the domains of innovation, space investigation, and maintainable energy. As the Chief of Tesla, Musk's authority style plays had a vital impact in the organization's development from an aggressive electric vehicle startup to a worldwide power molding the eventual fate of transportation and energy. Understanding Musk's authority style requires digging into the attributes that characterize his methodology, the difficulties he explored, and the significant effect he has had on Tesla's corporate culture.

One of Musk's characterizing authority characteristics is his nervy vision. Musk doesn't just hold back nothing; he focuses on groundbreaking, industry-rethinking objectives. This boldness was clear from the beginning of his inclusion with Tesla when he enunciated a mission to make electric vehicles as well as to speed up the world's change to feasible energy. Musk's vision reaches out past the prompt difficulties of building electric vehicles; it includes an all encompassing way to deal with address environmental change and reshape the energy scene.

Musk's initiative style is set apart by a persevering quest for aggressive objectives, frequently outlined as "moonshot" tries. The actual idea of efficiently manufacturing electric vehicles that are harmless to the ecosystem as well as superior execution and reasonable was a change in perspective in the auto business. This approach difficulties regular reasoning and has been a main thrust behind Tesla's capacity to disturb laid out standards.

Be that as it may, Musk's boldness isn't restricted to electric vehicles. His contribution in SpaceX, a confidential aviation producer and space transportation organization, embodies his penchant for great scope development. The objective of colonizing Mars, while apparently fantastical, encapsulates Musk's obligation to tending to mankind's drawn out endurance and broadening our span past Earth. This visionary standpoint rises above the limits of individual organizations, adding to a more extensive story of propelling human progress.

A critical part of Musk's authority style is his active contribution in the specialized parts of his endeavors. Musk, with a foundation in physical science and software engineering, has a profound comprehension of the designing and logical standards fundamental his organizations' items. This specialized astuteness recognizes him from numerous different Chiefs, permitting him to connect straightforwardly in critical thinking and dynamic cycles.

This active methodology was especially obvious during Tesla's initial years when Musk was profoundly associated with the turn of events and plan of the Roadster, Tesla's most memorable electric vehicle.

Musk's immediate association in tending to designing difficulties, refining vehicle plans, and enhancing execution added to the progress of the Roadster and set the vibe for future Tesla models.

Musk's initiative at SpaceX grandstands a comparative involved approach. From the improvement of the Bird of prey rockets to the aggressive Starship project, Musk is effectively associated with the specialized complexities of room investigation. His drenching in the designing subtleties empowers him to settle on informed choices, guide the advancement cycle, and explore the perplexing difficulties intrinsic in space investigation.

While Musk's specialized inclusion is a strength, it likewise presents difficulties. His active authority style has, on occasion, prompted a serious and requesting workplace. Reports of long work hours, elevated requirements, and a culture of tireless quest for objectives have surfaced, mirroring Musk's faithful obligation to his vision. This power, while driving advancement, has likewise started banters about balance between serious and fun activities and the prosperity of Tesla and SpaceX representatives.

An eminent feature of Musk's initiative style is his readiness to face huge individual challenges for the progress of his organizations. Musk contributed his very own significant measure capital into Tesla during its initial days, showing a degree of individual responsibility remarkable among Presidents. The monetary dangers he embraced highlighted his confidence in the mission and the likely effect of Tesla on the car business.

Additionally, Musk's authority process has been interlaced with monetary difficulties. Tesla, in its early stages, confronted doubt about its capacity to make money and accomplish long haul suitability. Musk's aggressive objectives, including efficiently manufacturing reasonable electric vehicles and building the Gigafactory for battery creation, confronted investigation from financial backers and industry specialists. Musk's own monetary ventures, combined with his capacity to get outside subsidizing, assumed an essential part in controlling Tesla through these monetary difficulties.

One more unmistakable part of Musk's initiative style is his straightforward and unfiltered correspondence, frequently worked with through virtual entertainment, especially Twitter. Musk's tweets have turned into a conspicuous element of his public persona, giving bits of knowledge into his reasoning, reports on organization improvements, and, on occasion, unfiltered articulations of disappointment or humor. This immediate and casual correspondence style has reverberated with many, cultivating a feeling of genuineness and straightforwardness.

Nonetheless, Musk's utilization of Twitter has not been without discussion. His tweets have, every so often, prompted market unpredictability, legitimate difficulties, and administrative examination. The crossing point of Musk's own correspondence and its effect on Tesla's stock costs has brought up issues about corporate administration and the obligations of Chiefs in the period of virtual entertainment.

Musk's correspondence style additionally stretches out to setting assumptions. His aggressive courses of events and striking expectations have become inseparable from his administration. The declaration of aggressive creation targets, courses of events for accomplishing Full Self-Driving (FSD) capacities, and disclosing new item includes have been signs of Musk's correspondence system. While these declarations produce fervor and drive a need to get a move on, they have likewise confronted wariness and examination, especially when courses of events are not met.

The turn of events and sending of Autopilot, Tesla's high level driver-help framework, represent Musk's way to deal with setting exclusive standards. The quest for independent driving capacities, verbalized through the FSD idea, has been a point of convergence of Tesla's development. In any case, accomplishing full independence in vehicles has demonstrated to be a perplexing test, prompting administrative examination and discussions about the innovation's status for boundless use.

Musk's initiative at Tesla has not been safe to inner and outside challenges. The securing of SolarCity, a sun based energy organization, in 2016, was met with doubt and monetary examination. Pundits scrutinized the essential reasoning behind the securing, and monetary tensions built as Tesla tried to incorporate SolarCity into its more extensive vision of a manageable energy biological system. Musk's capacity to explore these difficulties and adjust Tesla's plan of action exhibited strength even with monetary and key intricacies.

The debates encompassing Musk, from fights in court to conflicts with administrative specialists, have added layers of intricacy to his authority account. The legitimate settlement with the U.S. Protections and Trade Commission (SEC) over Musk's tweets about taking Tesla private highlighted the difficulties of offsetting individual correspondence with administrative commitments. Musk's eagerness to take part in fights in court, while intelligent of his determination, has provoked conversations about corporate administration and the obligations of high-profile Presidents.

In spite of the discussions, Musk's administration at Tesla has been instrumental in moving the organization to the front of the auto and energy businesses. His capacity to express a convincing vision, put forth aggressive objectives, and explore through difficulties has become inseparable from Tesla's corporate culture. Musk's strength, versatility, and ability to take on tremendous difficulties have made a permanent imprint on Tesla's direction and its part in forming the eventual fate of transportation and energy.

6.2 Analysis of Elon Musk's leadership principles.

Elon Musk's initiative standards, as shown through his job at Tesla and different endeavors, mirror an extraordinary mix of boldness, development, strength, and a steady quest for groundbreaking change. Breaking down Musk's initiative style divulges key rules that have formed his way to deal with directing Tesla from a beginning electric vehicle startup to a worldwide force to be reckoned with in practical transportation and energy.

At the center of Musk's initiative way of thinking is the rule of bold vision. Musk is prestigious for setting striking, industry-resisting objectives that rise above the norm. His vision goes past gradual enhancements; all things considered, he imagines progressive changes that can reshape whole ventures. This daringness was obvious right off the bat in Tesla's excursion when Musk enunciated a mission to create electric vehicles as well as to speed up the world's change to feasible energy.

The brassy vision isn't restricted to Tesla; it stretches out to Musk's association in SpaceX and different endeavors. The objective of colonizing Mars, for example, encapsulates Musk's obligation to handling humankind's most huge difficulties. This rule of boldness moves Musk and his organizations to take a stab at objectives that many should seriously mull over out of reach, cultivating a climate of nonstop development and pushing the limits of what is considered conceivable.

Couple with daring vision, Musk's administration standards underline active association in the specialized parts of his endeavors. Musk's experience in physical science and software engineering furnishes him with a profound comprehension of the designing and logical standards supporting the items created by his organizations. This involved methodology has been especially obvious in Musk's job at Tesla, where he has effectively taken part in critical thinking and dynamic cycles connected with vehicle configuration, designing difficulties, and mechanical progressions.

The specialized inundation isn't just representative; it is a substantial piece of Musk's initiative toolbox. His immediate contribution in critical thinking during the improvement of the Roadster, Tesla's most memorable electric vehicle, set a trend for future models. Musk's job in tending to designing difficulties and upgrading execution highlights the significance of specialized discernment in his administration style. This approach cultivates a culture of development and guarantees that the pioneer is personally familiar with the complexities of the items and innovations driving the organization forward.

An eminent rule in Musk's initiative collection is the readiness to face huge individual challenges for the outcome of his organizations. Musk's significant monetary interests in Tesla during its initial days displayed a degree of individual responsibility extraordinary among Presidents. This standard highlights Musk's confidence in the mission and the expected effect of Tesla on the car business and maintainable energy scene.

The monetary dangers attempted by Musk were not restricted to individual speculations; they reached out to getting outside subsidizing and guiding Tesla through times of monetary vulnerability. Musk's capacity to explore these difficulties and guarantee the monetary feasibility of Tesla mirrors an administration rule established in a profound obligation to the mission and a preparation to bear the weight of chance by and by.

Musk's initiative at Tesla is portrayed by a pledge to straightforwardness and unfiltered correspondence, frequently worked with through online entertainment, especially Twitter. This correspondence style, while eccentric, has turned into a characterizing component of Musk's public persona. Musk's tweets give bits of knowledge into his reasoning, reports on organization improvements, and unfiltered articulations of dissatisfaction or humor. This straightforward and direct correspondence style has reverberated with many, cultivating a feeling of credibility and transparency.

Nonetheless, this guideline of straightforward correspondence additionally presents difficulties. Musk's tweets have, now and again, prompted market instability, legitimate difficulties, and administrative investigation. The convergence of Musk's own correspondence and its effect on Tesla's stock costs has brought up issues about corporate administration and the obligations of Chiefs in the period of web-based entertainment. This standard features the double edged nature of straightforward correspondence and the requirement for balance among receptiveness and administrative consistence.

Musk's administration standards are intertwined with the setting of elevated requirements. His aggressive courses of events, striking forecasts, and declarations of notable advancements have become inseparable from his administration style. This standard of setting exclusive requirements fills various needs. It creates fervor, ingrains a need to get moving, and cultivates a culture of fast development. Be that as it may, it additionally welcomes examination, particularly when courses of events are not met or when the assumptions appear to be excessively hopeful.

The turn of events and sending of Autopilot, Tesla's high level driver-help framework, embody Musk's way to deal with setting elevated requirements. The quest for independent driving capacities, explained through the Full Self-Driving (FSD) idea, has been a point of convergence of Tesla's development. While this rule fills development, it additionally highlights the difficulties of overseeing assumptions and exploring the almost negligible difference between aggressive objectives and feasible achievements.

Flexibility is a focal fundamental of Musk's initiative standards. Tesla, under Musk's initiative, has confronted a bunch of difficulties, from monetary obstacles to creation delays and administrative investigation. Musk's strength even with these difficulties has been a characterizing factor in Tesla's capacity to weather conditions storms and arise more grounded. The capacity to adjust, gain from mishaps, and continue on chasing long haul objectives mirrors Musk's obligation to versatility as an initiative standard.

One of the remarkable difficulties that highlighted Musk's versatility was the obtaining of SolarCity in 2016. Regardless of incredulity and monetary investigation, Musk explored through the intricacies, adjusted Tesla's plan of action, and incorporated SolarCity into the more extensive vision of an economical energy environment.

This versatility despite monetary and vital moves exhibits Musk's obligation to the drawn out mission and the capacity to turn in light of evolving conditions.

Musk's initiative standards stretch out past Tesla to adventures like SpaceX and The Exhausting Organization. The overall guideline here is an eagerness to take on huge difficulties with worldwide importance. The objective of colonizing Mars and the improvement of the Hyperloop transportation idea represent Musk's hunger for extraordinary change on a planetary scale. These endeavors, while unmistakable from Tesla, add to a more extensive story of propelling human progress and tending to a portion of mankind's most squeezing difficulties.

Be that as it may, Musk's authority style isn't without debate. His frank and in some cases flighty conduct via online entertainment has drawn both deference and analysis. Musk's utilization of Twitter, specifically, has prompted market instability, lawful difficulties, and administrative examination. The public persona of Musk, frequently depicted through his tweets and communications, adds a layer of intricacy to his initiative story.

The contentions encompassing Musk, from his public assertions to fights in court and conflicts with administrative specialists, highlight the difficulties of driving an organization as unique and powerful as Tesla. The double job of Musk as both Chief and an individual of note with a critical online entertainment presence adds a layer of intricacy to Tesla's corporate administration and brings up issues about the crossing point of individual and corporate initiative.

6.3 Decisions that defined Tesla's trajectory.

Tesla's direction, from its initial days as an earth shattering startup to its flow status as a worldwide forerunner in electric vehicles and reasonable energy, has been molded by a progression of urgent choices. These choices, frequently determined by the dauntlessness and vision of Chief Elon Musk and the organization's authority group, have characterized Tesla's way, affecting its item arrangement, business techniques, and its effect on the auto and energy ventures. Inspecting the key choices that have denoted Tesla's process gives experiences into the elements that have moved its prosperity and reshaped the scene of transportation and energy.

One of the primary choices that set Tesla on its direction was the vision to rethink electric vehicles. In the mid 2000s, electric vehicles were to a great extent saw as unrealistic and ailing in execution, with restricted claim past a specialty market. Nonetheless, Tesla's pioneers, Martin Eberhard and Marc Tarpenning, imagined electric vehicles as something other than naturally cognizant transportation. They looked to make electric vehicles that could match customary gas powered motor vehicles with regards to execution, attractiveness, and openness.

The choice to zero in on elite execution electric vehicles was solidified with the improvement of the Tesla Roadster, the organization's most memorable creation vehicle. Presented in 2008, the Roadster exhibited the capability of electric impetus in an elite execution sports vehicle.

It was not just an electric vehicle; it was an explanation that electric vehicles could be invigorating, quick, and alluring. This choice tested the common account about electric vehicles, laying the preparation for Tesla's future undertakings.

Elon Musk's entrance into Tesla in 2004 denoted another crucial choice point. Musk, definitely known for his prosperity with PayPal and his visionary viewpoint with SpaceX, carried a groundbreaking vision to Tesla. His choice to put individual capital in the organization and expect a position of authority denoted a defining moment. Musk mixed truly necessary monetary assets as well as expressed a mission that went past building electric vehicles.

Musk's choice to grow Tesla's main goal to speed up the world's progress to practical energy turned into a core value. This choice expanded the extent of Tesla's desires, enveloping electric vehicles as well as an exhaustive vision for a practical energy biological system. Musk's initiative and dynamic style, described by dauntlessness and an eagerness to handle worldwide difficulties, established the groundwork for Tesla's development into a complex player in the auto and energy areas.

The presentation of the Model S in 2012 was a choice that fundamentally formed Tesla's direction. The Model S, an all-electric extravagance car, addressed a takeoff from the Roadster and denoted Tesla's entrance into the standard car market. The choice to create an extravagance car was vital, situating Tesla in a portion where it could exhibit the capacities of electric impetus while engaging a more extensive client base.

The Model S got far reaching recognition for its plan, execution, and long-range abilities. It showed the way that electric vehicles couldn't coordinate however outperform customary extravagance vehicles in key credits. This choice to deliver an extravagance electric car not just cemented Tesla's situation in the car business yet additionally produced income that would be vital for future extension and improvement.

The choice to construct the Gigafactory, declared in 2014, was an essential move that addressed basic difficulties connected with battery creation. Batteries are a crucial part of electric vehicles, and their expense and accessibility were critical hindrances to far and wide reception. The Gigafactory, situated in Nevada, was intended to deliver batteries at an uncommon scale, driving down expenses and supporting Tesla's objective of efficiently manufacturing reasonable electric vehicles.

The Gigafactory choice was not just about scale; it was about vertical coordination and command over a critical part of Tesla's items. By delivering its own batteries, Tesla diminished reliance on outside providers, moderated store network chances, and acquired an upper hand with regards to cost proficiency. This choice exhibited Tesla's obligation to tending to the difficulties obstructing the inescapable reception of electric vehicles.

The Model 3, presented in 2017, denoted a groundbreaking choice that expected to carry electric vehicles to the mass market. The choice to deliver a more reasonable electric vehicle lined up with Tesla's central goal to speed up the progress to manageable energy. The Model 3 was situated as a vehicle that could speak to a more extensive scope of customers, making electric vehicles open to a bigger portion of the populace.

The creation challenges related with the Model 3, frequently alluded to as "creation damnation," featured the intricacies of increasing assembling to satisfy high need. This choice to target mass-market reception brought the two valuable open doors and difficulties. While the creation obstacles gathered huge consideration, the choice to focus on moderateness and creation versatility highlighted Tesla's obligation to settling on electric vehicles a standard decision.

The choice to propose over-the-air (OTA) programming refreshes for Tesla vehicles denoted a change in outlook in the auto business. Dissimilar to customary automakers, Tesla's choice to use OTA refreshes permitted the organization to send updates to its vehicles from a distance. This choice, established in programming driven thinking, presented a dynamic and iterative way to deal with vehicle usefulness, execution, and wellbeing.

The OTA update capacity has turned into a sign of Tesla's way to deal with consistent improvement. It empowers the organization to resolve issues, improve execution, and present new highlights without requiring actual visits to support focuses. This choice lines up with Tesla's ethos of quick cycle and flexibility, attributes more usually connected with innovation organizations than conventional automakers.

The procurement of SolarCity in 2016 was a choice that lengthy Tesla's impression into the energy area. SolarCity, a sun powered energy organization helped to establish by Musk's cousins, worked in sun powered chargers and energy administrations. The choice to gain SolarCity was met with doubt and monetary examination, as pundits scrutinized the essential reasoning and possible irreconcilable circumstances.

In any case, Musk imagined a comprehensive energy biological system where electric vehicles, energy capacity, and sun based energy arrangements would synergistically cooperate. This choice meant to situate Tesla as a thorough supplier of feasible energy arrangements, tending to both transportation and energy needs. In spite of the contentions, the choice to coordinate SolarCity into Tesla's portfolio mirrored Musk's drawn out vision for a supportable energy future.

The choice to create and send Autopilot, Tesla's high level driver-help framework, denoted an introduction to independent driving innovation. Autopilot, presented in 2015, exhibited Tesla's obligation to pushing the limits of vehicle robotization. The choice to offer semi-independent highlights lined up with Musk's vision of accomplishing Full Self-Driving (FSD) capacity later on.

The Autopilot choice, while exhibiting Tesla's innovative ability, likewise brought difficulties. The quest for independence confronted administrative investigation, security concerns, and discussions about the availability of such innovation for boundless use. This choice highlighted the harmony among advancement and dependable organization, featuring the intricacies of presenting state of the art innovation in the car business.

The choice to uncover and acknowledge pre-orders for the Cybertruck in 2019 was a striking move that displayed Tesla's readiness to challenge ordinary plan standards. The Cybertruck, with its unpredictable, rakish plan, denoted a takeoff from conventional pickup truck feel. The choice to embrace a polarizing configuration mirrored Musk's tendency to upset laid out standards and take special care of shoppers searching for an exceptional and modern vehicle.

The Cybertruck choice produced critical public consideration as well as flagged Tesla's entrance into the profoundly worthwhile pickup truck market. This choice featured Tesla's capacity to expect market patterns, grasp customer inclinations, and enhance in a fragment overwhelmed by customary automakers.

The choice to enter the energy stockpiling market with the Powerwall, Powerpack, and Megapack was an essential move that extended Tesla's impact past electric vehicles. The Powerwall, presented in 2015, is a private energy stockpiling arrangement that permits property holders to store overabundance energy produced by sunlight based chargers. The Powerpack and Megapack target business and utility-scale energy capacity.

This choice lined up with Tesla's more extensive vision of making an economical energy biological system. By giving energy stockpiling arrangements, Tesla intended to address the irregular idea of environmentally friendly power sources, upgrading the unwavering quality and steadiness of sustainable power frameworks. The choice to expand into energy capacity displayed Tesla's obligation to molding the eventual fate of both transportation and energy.

The choice to enter the Chinese market with the development of Gigafactory Shanghai was an essential move that situated Tesla as a key part on the planet's biggest auto market. The Chinese market introduced monstrous open doors, yet in addition challenges, including administrative intricacies and rivalry from neighborhood makers. The choice to lay out neighborhood creation in China was pointed toward taking advantage of the developing interest for electric vehicles in the area.

6.4 The intersection of Musk's vision and corporate culture.

The convergence of Elon Musk's visionary authority and the corporate culture at Tesla is a powerful scene that plays had a vital impact in forming the organization's character, driving development, and exploring difficulties. Musk's visionary standpoint, described by daringness and a guarantee to groundbreaking change, has become entwined with the way of life at Tesla, impacting its qualities, dynamic cycles, and the quest for aggressive objectives.

At the core of this crossing point is Musk's brassy vision for what's to come. His overall objective, verbalized from the beginning of his association with Tesla, is to speed up the world's progress to manageable energy. This vision reaches out past the creation of electric vehicles; it envelops an all encompassing way to deal with address environmental change, change the energy scene, and eventually impel humankind towards a more reasonable future.

The arrangement of Musk's vision with Tesla's corporate culture is obvious in the organization's statement of purpose: "To speed up the world's progress to reasonable energy." This mission fills in as a core value that saturates the association's ethos, impacting vital choices, item improvement, and the general heading of the organization. The collaboration between Musk's vision and Tesla's central goal makes a feeling of direction that heads past the conventional extent of an auto organization.

The venturesome objectives set by Musk, from efficiently manufacturing reasonable electric vehicles to colonizing Mars, have become piece of Tesla's DNA. The corporate culture at Tesla flourishes with the quest for aggressive goals that rock the boat. This culture of pushing limits and embracing boldness has energized development, cultivating a mentality that urges workers to think past customary cutoff points and investigate groundbreaking thoughts.

One of the main traits of Musk's vision is the accentuation on quick advancement and emphasis. This standard is implanted in Tesla's way to deal with item improvement and innovation sending. The organization's obligation to over-the-air programming refreshes for its vehicles embodies this attitude. Tesla's vehicles are not static; they advance and work on after some time as programming refreshes present new highlights, improve execution, and address issues.

The crossing point of Musk's vision and Tesla's way of life of quick cycle is especially apparent in the improvement of Autopilot, Tesla's high level driver-help framework. The choice to seek after independence in vehicles lines up with Musk's more extensive vision of a future where transportation isn't just economical yet additionally more secure and more proficient. The iterative way to deal with Autopilot mirrors a guarantee to constant improvement and the conviction that innovation can assume an essential part in propelling the car business.

Besides, Musk's emphasis on vertical incorporation lines up with Tesla's corporate culture of controlling key parts of the creation cycle. The choice to construct the Gigafactory for battery creation, for example, was not just about scale; it was tied in with applying command over a basic part of Tesla's items. This obligation to vertical joining is established in the conviction that having more prominent command over the production network is fundamental for driving down costs, guaranteeing quality, and keeping an upper hand.

The crossing point of Musk's vision and Tesla's way of life is additionally apparent in the organization's introduction to energy items. The procurement of SolarCity and the improvement of energy stockpiling arrangements like the Powerwall and Powerpack feature a promise to a far reaching energy biological system.

Musk's vision of a future fueled by manageable energy stretches out past vehicles to incorporate private and business energy arrangements. This comprehensive way to deal with tending to energy challenges is intelligent of Tesla's corporate culture of reasoning expansively about its part in molding an economical future.

Be that as it may, the convergence of Musk's vision and corporate culture isn't without challenges. The aggressive courses of events set by Musk, frequently conveyed through web-based entertainment, have been a wellspring of both motivation and distrust. The strain to fulfill forceful time constraints, combined with the quick moving nature of development, has prompted banters about possibility and the potential compromises among speed and exhaustive testing.

Moreover, the power and requesting nature of Musk's initiative style have been both a wellspring of inspiration and a disputed matter. Reports of long work hours, exclusive requirements, and a culture of persevering quest for objectives have brought up issues about balance between fun and serious activities and representative prosperity. The crossing point of Musk's own drive and Tesla's corporate culture possibly affects the organization's labor force.

The job of straightforward correspondence in the convergence of Musk's vision and Tesla's corporate culture is a situation with two sides. Musk's utilization of web-based entertainment, especially Twitter, to discuss straightforwardly with general society has brought a degree of straightforwardness and credibility to Tesla's story. Notwithstanding, it has additionally prompted market unpredictability, legitimate difficulties, and administrative examination. The casual and unfiltered nature of Musk's correspondence style features the difficulties of offsetting straightforwardness with the obligations of a public corporation.

The convergence of Musk's vision and corporate culture is likewise apparent in Tesla's commitment with the more extensive cultural talk. Musk's public position on issues, for example, ecological maintainability, environmental change, and the job of innovation in molding what's in store mirrors a corporate culture that looks to be a member as well as a forerunner in conversations that influence the world at large.

The effect of this convergence goes past the bounds of Tesla's central command. It reaches out to the more extensive environment of providers, accomplices, and clients who are important for the organization's vision for a practical future. The reception of electric vehicles, progressions in energy capacity, and the quest for independence in vehicles are features of this more extensive effect. Tesla's effect on the car and energy ventures is a demonstration of the crossing point of Musk's visionary initiative and the corporate culture that impels the organization forward.

Chapter 7

Financial Rollercoaster

Tesla's process has been set apart by a monetary rollercoaster, a unique ride that mirrors the highs of development, market energy, and key triumphs, combined with the lows of creation challenges, administrative examination, and periodic disturbance in the monetary business sectors. Understanding the monetary direction of Tesla requires digging into the organization's initial battles, its extraordinary victories, and the continuous moves that keep on molding its monetary account.

In the beginning of Tesla's monetary story, the organization confronted impressive difficulties. Established in 2003, Tesla Engines (as it was known at that point) was wandering into a car scene overwhelmed by laid out monsters with many years of involvement. The electric vehicle market, by then, was specialty, with distrust about the suitability and mass allure of electric vehicles. Tesla's initial monetary battles were highlighted by the advancement of its most memorable creation vehicle, the Tesla Roadster.

The Roadster, presented in 2008, was Tesla's initial introduction to the car market. While it exhibited the capability of electric impetus, its creation was laden with difficulties. Significant expenses, low creation volumes, and the utilization of parts from different providers made a monetary burden on the organization. The Roadster project, while pivotal in showing the capacities of electric vehicles, featured the monetary delicacy of a beginning Tesla.

During this early period, Tesla's monetary circumstance was dubious. The organization confronted income issues, battled with creation delays, and experienced suspicion from both industry onlookers and possible clients. The monetary rollercoaster took a critical turn when Elon Musk, currently a vital financial backer in Tesla, expected a more straightforward position of authority and put extra private assets into the organization. Musk's monetary responsibility flagged areas of strength for an in the mission and expected outcome of Tesla, giving a life saver during a basic stage.

The monetary account moved with the presentation of the Model S in 2012. Situated as an extravagance electric car, the Model S planned to show the way that electric vehicles couldn't contend however outperform customary extravagance vehicles in execution, plan, and attractiveness. The Model S got far and wide recognition, winning honors and catching the consideration of buyers who had not recently viewed as electric vehicles.

The outcome of the Model S had significant ramifications for Tesla's monetary viewpoint. The positive gathering supported request, empowering Tesla to accomplish a degree of monetary soundness that had escaped the organization in its initial years. The monetary rollercoaster, once portrayed by vulnerability, started to rise as Tesla cut a specialty in the extravagance electric vehicle market.

Urgently, Tesla's monetary rollercoaster was additionally moved by the choice to open up to the world in 2010. The first sale of stock (Initial public offering) denoted an extraordinary second, furnishing Tesla with much-required capital and a public stage. The Initial public offering, be that as it may, was not without challenges. Tesla turned into the primary American carmaker to open up to the world since Portage in 1956, and suspicion about the electric vehicle market waited among financial backers.

The period following the Initial public offering saw Tesla's stock encountering instability, intelligent of the innate vulnerability encompassing an organization with aggressive objectives and problematic innovation. The monetary rollercoaster went on with fluctuating stock costs, an impression of both market opinion and the story around Tesla's development possibilities.

Tesla's monetary direction took a critical positive turn with the declaration of the Gigafactory in 2014. The Gigafactory, an enormous office committed to the development of batteries, planned to address one of the basic difficulties confronting the electric vehicle industry — battery costs. By accomplishing economies of scale through the Gigafactory, Tesla looked to drive down the expense of batteries, making electric vehicles more reasonable and economical.

The monetary effect of the Gigafactory choice was multi-layered. It addressed an intense move to control a pivotal part of Tesla's inventory network, decreasing reliance on outside providers and moderating dangers related with the worldwide battery market. The Gigafactory likewise flagged Tesla's obligation to large scale manufacturing, with the expectation to deliver batteries at a scale that could uphold the aggressive creation objectives for the impending Model 3.

The uncovering of the Model 3 out of 2016 denoted a turning point in Tesla's monetary story. Situated as a more reasonable electric car, the Model 3 intended to carry electric vehicles to a more extensive customer base. The declaration of the Model 3 gathered huge public premium, with countless pre-orders flooding in, joined by a flood in Tesla's market capitalization.

Nonetheless, the creation challenges that followed tried Tesla's monetary flexibility. The organization confronted what Elon Musk alluded to as "creation damnation," experiencing deferrals, bottlenecks, and strategic difficulties in the increase of Model

3 creation. The monetary rollercoaster went all in as Tesla battled to satisfy the significant need while wrestling with the intricacies of increasing assembling.

Tesla's capacity to explore this time of creation challenges exhibited its flexibility. The organization executed methodologies to smooth out creation, address bottlenecks, and enhance productivity on the manufacturing plant floor. Musk's involved contribution in critical thinking highlighted a guarantee to beating impediments and following through on the commitments made to clients and financial backers.

The monetary rollercoaster rose by and by as Tesla effectively conquered the creation obstacles. The Model 3 turned into a huge driver of Tesla's income, adding to the organization's progress from a specialty player to a mass-market electric vehicle producer. The effective creation and conveyance of the Model 3 supported Tesla's monetary exhibition as well as hardened its situation as a central part in the auto business.

Tesla's monetary direction kept on moving with vital moves into energy items. The obtaining of SolarCity in 2016 denoted a huge step into the sun oriented energy area. Notwithstanding, the choice was met with discussion, with pundits scrutinizing the essential reasoning and possible irreconcilable situations, given Musk's connections to SolarCity. The monetary mix of SolarCity into Tesla was not without challenges, and the move drew investigation from financial backers and administrative specialists.

The monetary rollercoaster went off in strange directions with Musk's declaration in 2018 that he was thinking about taking Tesla private. The tweet, communicating Musk's disappointment with the examination and tensions of being a public corporation, set off a whirlwind of reactions, lawful examinations, and changes in Tesla's stock cost. The episode featured the intricacies of exploring the convergence of corporate authority, individual correspondence, and market elements.

Regardless of the choppiness encompassing the go-private tweet, Tesla stayed a public corporation. The monetary rollercoaster went on with a progression of triumphs and difficulties, including the send off of new vehicle models, headways in independent driving innovation, and the disclosing of the Cybertruck. Every improvement impacted Tesla's monetary account, adding to its fairly estimated worth and molding view of the organization's future direction.

The monetary story went off in one more strange direction with Musk's declaration in 2021 that Tesla had put $1.5 billion in Bitcoin and would acknowledge the digital currency as installment for its vehicles.

The move pointed out the convergence of innovation, money, and Musk's unusual way to deal with business. In any case, the choice likewise started banters about the ecological effect of Bitcoin mining, prompting Musk later declaring that Tesla would never again acknowledge Bitcoin because of natural worries.

The monetary rollercoaster was additionally highlighted by Tesla's consideration in the S&P 500 file in 2020. This noticeable a critical approval of Tesla's height as a central part in the securities exchange and a groundbreaking power in the car and energy ventures. The consideration in the S&P 500 brought expanded perceivability, however it likewise acquainted Tesla with another arrangement of difficulties related with uplifted examination from institutional financial backers.

7.1 Tesla's Financial Journey

Tesla's monetary excursion has been an enrapturing adventure, set apart by development, flexibility, and a progression of key choices that have formed the organization's direction in the auto and energy areas. From its initial battles to secure itself in the electric vehicle market to turning into a central part with a huge effect on worldwide ventures, Tesla's monetary story mirrors the powerful idea of both the organization and the business sectors it works in.

In the beginning of Tesla's monetary excursion, the organization confronted impressive difficulties. Established in 2003 by Martin Eberhard and Marc Tarpenning, Tesla entered a car scene overwhelmed by laid out monsters with many years of involvement. The overall wariness about the practicality and mass allure of electric vehicles added an extra layer of trouble. Tesla's underlying monetary battles were articulated during the turn of events and creation of its most memorable creation vehicle, the Tesla Roadster.

Presented in 2008, the Roadster was a historic electric games vehicle that displayed the capability of electric impetus. Be that as it may, its creation was laden with difficulties. Significant expenses, low creation volumes, and the utilization of parts from different providers made a monetary stress on the organization. The Roadster project, while spearheading in exhibiting the capacities of electric vehicles, highlighted the monetary delicacy of a beginning Tesla.

During this early period, Tesla confronted income issues, battled with creation delays, and experienced distrust from both industry onlookers and expected clients. The monetary rollercoaster took a huge turn when Elon Musk, currently a critical financial backer in Tesla, expected a more straightforward position of authority and put extra private assets into the organization. Musk's monetary responsibility flagged areas of strength for an in the mission and expected progress of Tesla, giving a urgent life saver during a basic stage.

The monetary direction started to move with the presentation of the Model S in 2012. Situated as an extravagance electric car, the Model S planned to show the way that electric vehicles couldn't contend yet outperform conventional extravagance vehicles in execution, plan, and allure. The Model S got far and wide approval, winning honors and catching the consideration of purchasers who had not recently viewed as electric vehicles.

The outcome of the Model S had significant ramifications for Tesla's monetary viewpoint. The positive gathering supported request, empowering Tesla to accomplish a degree of monetary soundness that had evaded the organization in its initial years. The monetary rollercoaster, once portrayed by vulnerability, started to rise as Tesla cut a specialty in the extravagance electric vehicle market.

Urgently, Tesla's monetary rollercoaster was additionally moved by the choice to open up to the world in 2010. The first sale of stock (Initial public offering) denoted an extraordinary second, giving Tesla much-required capital and a public stage. The Initial public offering, in any case, was not without challenges. Tesla turned into the main American carmaker to open up to the world since Portage in 1956, and doubt about the electric vehicle market waited among financial backers.

The period following the Initial public offering saw Tesla's stock encountering instability, intelligent of the intrinsic vulnerability encompassing an organization with aggressive objectives and troublesome innovation. The monetary rollercoaster went on with fluctuating stock costs, an impression of both market opinion and the story around Tesla's development possibilities.

Tesla's monetary direction took a huge positive turn with the declaration of the Gigafactory in 2014. The Gigafactory, a gigantic office devoted to the creation of batteries, planned to address one of the basic difficulties confronting the electric vehicle industry — battery costs. By accomplishing economies of scale through the Gigafactory, Tesla looked to drive down the expense of batteries, making electric vehicles more reasonable and economical.

The monetary effect of the Gigafactory choice was diverse. It addressed an intense move to control a pivotal part of Tesla's inventory network, diminishing reliance on outer providers and moderating dangers related with the worldwide battery market. The Gigafactory likewise flagged Tesla's obligation to large scale manufacturing, with the purpose to deliver batteries at a scale that could uphold the aggressive creation objectives for the impending Model 3.

The disclosing of the Model 3 out of 2016 denoted a turning point in Tesla's monetary story. Situated as a more reasonable electric car, the Model 3 expected to carry electric vehicles to a more extensive customer base. The declaration of the Model 3 earned gigantic public premium, with countless pre-orders flooding in, joined by a flood in Tesla's market capitalization.

Notwithstanding, the creation challenges that followed tried Tesla's monetary strength. The organization confronted what Elon Musk alluded to as "creation damnation," experiencing postponements, bottlenecks, and strategic difficulties in the increase of Model 3 creation. The monetary rollercoaster went all in as Tesla battled to satisfy the serious need while wrestling with the intricacies of increasing assembling.

Tesla's capacity to explore this time of creation challenges displayed its flexibility. The organization executed methodologies to smooth out creation, address bottlenecks, and streamline effectiveness on the processing plant floor. Musk's active contribution in critical thinking highlighted a guarantee to defeating impediments and following through on the commitments made to clients and financial backers.

Yet again the monetary rollercoaster climbed as Tesla effectively defeated the creation obstacles. The Model 3 turned into a critical driver of Tesla's income, adding to the organization's progress from a specialty player to a mass-market electric vehicle producer. The effective creation and conveyance of the Model 3 helped Tesla's monetary presentation as well as cemented its situation as a central part in the auto business.

Tesla's monetary direction kept on moving with vital moves into energy items. The securing of SolarCity in 2016 denoted a critical stage into the sun oriented energy area. Be that as it may, the choice was met with contention, with pundits scrutinizing the essential reasoning and likely irreconcilable circumstances, given Musk's connections to SolarCity. The monetary coordination of SolarCity into Tesla was not without challenges, and the move drew investigation from financial backers and administrative specialists.

The monetary rollercoaster veered off in strange directions with Musk's declaration in 2018 that he was thinking about taking Tesla private. The tweet, communicating Musk's dissatisfaction with the examination and tensions of being a public corporation, set off a whirlwind of reactions, lawful examinations, and variances in Tesla's stock cost. The episode featured the intricacies of exploring the crossing point of corporate authority, individual correspondence, and market elements.

In spite of the choppiness encompassing the go-private tweet, Tesla stayed a public corporation. The monetary rollercoaster went on with a progression of victories and difficulties, including the send off of new vehicle models, headways in independent driving innovation, and the revealing of the Cybertruck. Every advancement impacted Tesla's monetary account, adding to its reasonable worth and forming impression of the organization's future direction.

The monetary story veered off in one more strange direction with Musk's declaration in 2021 that Tesla had put $1.5 billion in Bitcoin and would acknowledge the cryptographic money as installment for its vehicles. The move pointed out the convergence of innovation, money, and Musk's capricious way to deal with business.

In any case, the choice likewise ignited banters about the ecological effect of Bitcoin mining, prompting Musk later declaring that Tesla would never again acknowledge Bitcoin because of natural worries.

The monetary rollercoaster was additionally complemented by Tesla's consideration in the S&P 500 record in 2020. This noticeable a critical approval of Tesla's height as a key part in the financial exchange and a groundbreaking power in the car and energy enterprises. The consideration in the S&P 500 brought expanded perceivability, however it likewise acquainted Tesla with another arrangement of difficulties related with elevated examination from institutional financial backers.

The monetary rollercoaster arrived at new levels as Tesla's market capitalization took off, making it one of the most important organizations worldwide. The flood in Tesla's stock cost reflected financial backer trust in the organization's capacity to reform the auto business, advance electric vehicle innovation, and rethink energy arrangements. Notwithstanding, the fleeting ascent additionally welcomed incredulity and discussions about the supportability of Tesla's valuation.

In the midst of the monetary highs, Tesla kept on confronting difficulties connected with creation versatility, administrative examination, and the intricacies of dealing with a worldwide production network. The organization's venture into new business sectors, including China, further added layers of intricacy to its monetary tasks. The Shanghai Gigafactory, introduced in 2019, addressed an essential move to take advantage of the blossoming electric vehicle market in China, however it likewise involved exploring administrative systems, international contemplations, and rivalry from nearby producers.

Tesla's monetary excursion likewise converged with banters about corporate administration and the job of Musk as both Chief and a huge investor. The power of Musk's contribution in everyday tasks, his immediate correspondence with general society through online entertainment, and periodic debates brought up issues about the conventional standards of corporate administration. Musk's effect on Tesla's monetary story went past conventional measurements, stretching out to the domain of brand.

7.2 Overview of Tesla's financial ups and downs.

Tesla's monetary excursion has been a rollercoaster ride, described by emotional ups and testing downs, mirroring the intricacies and dynamism of the auto and energy enterprises. The outline of Tesla's monetary high points and low points gives experiences into the extraordinary occasions, key choices, and outside factors that have formed the organization's monetary account throughout the long term.

In the early long stretches of Tesla, the organization confronted critical monetary difficulties. Laid out in 2003, Tesla entered a car scene overwhelmed by conventional makers with many years of involvement.

The electric vehicle market, at that point, was a specialty section with suspicion about the practicality and mass allure of electric vehicles. Tesla's monetary battles were obvious during the turn of events and creation of its most memorable creation vehicle, the Tesla Roadster.

Presented in 2008, the Roadster was an earth shattering electric games vehicle that exhibited the capability of electric impetus. In any case, its creation was damaged by difficulties like significant expenses, low creation volumes, and dependence on parts from different providers. This overwhelmed the organization, featuring the troubles looked by a youngster electric vehicle maker in a cutthroat and laid out industry.

During this underlying period, Tesla wrestled with income issues, creation postponements, and incredulity from both industry eyewitnesses and possible clients. The monetary standpoint took a turn when Elon Musk, currently a vital financial backer in Tesla, expected a more straightforward influential position and infused extra private assets into the organization. Musk's monetary responsibility flagged areas of strength for an in the mission and likely outcome of Tesla, giving a significant life saver during a basic stage.

The monetary direction started to move with the presentation of the Model S in 2012. This extravagance electric car expected to rethink the impression of electric vehicles by unbelievable conventional extravagance vehicles in execution, plan, and allure. The Model S got far reaching approval, winning honors and catching the consideration of customers who had not recently viewed as electric vehicles.

The outcome of the Model S had significant ramifications for Tesla's monetary standing. The positive gathering helped request, empowering Tesla to accomplish a degree of monetary strength that had escaped the organization in its initial years. The monetary rollercoaster, once described by vulnerability, started to rise as Tesla laid down a good foundation for itself as a player in the extravagance electric vehicle market.

Significantly, Tesla's monetary rollercoaster was additionally filled by the choice to open up to the world in 2010. The first sale of stock (Initial public offering) denoted a groundbreaking second, giving Tesla much-required capital and a public stage. The Initial public offering, in any case, was not without challenges. Tesla turned into the principal American carmaker to open up to the world since Passage in 1956, and suspicion about the electric vehicle market waited among financial backers.

The period following the Initial public offering saw Tesla's stock encountering instability, mirroring the inborn vulnerability encompassing an organization with aggressive objectives and troublesome innovation. The monetary rollercoaster went on with fluctuating stock costs, affected by both market feeling and the story around Tesla's development possibilities.

Tesla's monetary direction took a huge positive turn with the declaration of the Gigafactory in 2014. The Gigafactory, devoted to the creation of batteries, expected to address a basic test confronting the electric vehicle industry — battery costs. By accomplishing economies of scale through the Gigafactory, Tesla expected to drive down the expense of batteries, making electric vehicles more reasonable and manageable.

The monetary effect of the Gigafactory choice was diverse. It addressed an intense move to control an essential part of Tesla's inventory network, diminishing reliance on outer providers and relieving gambles related with the worldwide battery market. The Gigafactory likewise flagged Tesla's obligation to large scale manufacturing, with the aim to deliver batteries at a scale that could uphold the aggressive creation objectives for the impending Model 3.

The disclosing of the Model 3 of every 2016 denoted a urgent second in Tesla's monetary story. Situated as a more reasonable electric car, the Model 3 planned to carry electric vehicles to a more extensive customer base. The declaration of the Model 3 earned gigantic public premium, with a huge number of pre-orders flooding in, joined by a flood in Tesla's market capitalization.

Nonetheless, the creation challenges that followed tried Tesla's monetary strength. The organization confronted what Elon Musk alluded to as "creation damnation," experiencing deferrals, bottlenecks, and strategic difficulties in the increase of Model 3 creation. The monetary rollercoaster dived in as Tesla battled to satisfy the significant need while wrestling with the intricacies of increasing assembling.

Tesla's capacity to explore this time of creation challenges displayed its flexibility. The organization carried out procedures to smooth out creation, address bottlenecks, and advance proficiency on the plant floor. Musk's involved contribution in critical thinking highlighted a pledge to conquering deterrents and following through on the commitments made to clients and financial backers.

Once more the monetary rollercoaster climbed as Tesla effectively defeated the creation obstacles. The Model 3 turned into a critical driver of Tesla's income, adding to the organization's change from a specialty player to a mass-market electric vehicle maker. The effective creation and conveyance of the Model 3 helped Tesla's monetary exhibition as well as hardened its situation as a key part in the car business.

Tesla's monetary direction kept on moving with vital moves into energy items. The obtaining of SolarCity in 2016 denoted a huge step into the sunlight based energy area. Be that as it may, the choice was met with contention, with pundits scrutinizing the essential reasoning and likely irreconcilable circumstances, given Musk's connections to SolarCity. The monetary coordination of SolarCity into Tesla was not without challenges, and the move drew investigation from financial backers and administrative specialists.

The monetary rollercoaster veered off in strange directions with Musk's declaration in 2018 that he was thinking about taking Tesla private. The tweet, communicating Musk's dissatisfaction with the examination and tensions of being a public corporation, set off a whirlwind of reactions, lawful examinations, and variances in Tesla's stock cost. The episode featured the intricacies of exploring the crossing point of corporate administration, individual correspondence, and market elements.

In spite of the disturbance encompassing the go-private tweet, Tesla stayed a public corporation. The monetary rollercoaster went on with a progression of victories and difficulties, including the send off of new vehicle models, headways in independent driving innovation, and the divulging of the Cybertruck. Every improvement impacted Tesla's monetary story, adding to its reasonable worth and forming impression of the organization's future direction.

The monetary account veered off in one more strange direction with Musk's declaration in 2021 that Tesla had put $1.5 billion in Bitcoin and would acknowledge the cryptographic money as installment for its vehicles. The move focused on the convergence of innovation, money, and Musk's unpredictable way to deal with business. In any case, the choice additionally ignited banters about the ecological effect of Bitcoin mining, prompting Musk later reporting that Tesla would never again acknowledge Bitcoin because of natural worries.

The monetary rollercoaster was additionally emphasizd by Tesla's consideration in the S&P 500 record in 2020. This noticeable a critical approval of Tesla's height as a central part in the securities exchange and a groundbreaking power in the auto and energy ventures. The consideration in the S&P 500 brought expanded perceivability, yet it likewise acquainted Tesla with another arrangement of difficulties related with uplifted examination from institutional financial backers.

The monetary rollercoaster arrived at new levels as Tesla's market capitalization took off, making it one of the most significant organizations around the world. The flood in Tesla's stock cost reflected financial backer trust in the organization's capacity to upset the auto business, advance electric vehicle innovation, and rethink energy arrangements. Nonetheless, the fleeting ascent additionally welcomed suspicion and discussions about the maintainability of Tesla's valuation.

In the midst of the monetary highs, Tesla kept on confronting difficulties connected with creation versatility, administrative examination, and the intricacies of dealing with a worldwide store network. The organization's venture into new business sectors, including China, further added layers of intricacy to its monetary activities. The Shanghai Gigafactory, introduced in 2019, addressed an essential move to take advantage of the thriving electric vehicle market in China, however it likewise involved exploring administrative structures, international contemplations, and rivalry from nearby makers.

Tesla's monetary excursion likewise crossed with banters about corporate administration and the job of Musk as both Chief and a huge investor. The force of Musk's contribution in everyday activities, his immediate correspondence with people in general through online entertainment, and periodic contentions brought up issues about the customary standards of corporate administration. Musk's effect on Tesla's monetary story went past customary measurements, reaching out to the domain of brand insight, market feeling, and public talk.

7.3 Factors influencing the company's financial standing.

Tesla's monetary standing is impacted by a large number of elements, mirroring the complexities of the auto and energy ventures, worldwide financial circumstances, administrative scenes, and the powerful idea of mechanical development. As an organization that works at the convergence of state of the art innovation and manageable arrangements, Tesla's monetary direction is molded by a mix of inward methodologies, outer market influences, and the extraordinary vision of its initiative.

One of the urgent elements affecting Tesla's monetary standing is its item portfolio. The achievement and interest for Tesla's electric vehicles (EVs) assume a focal part in deciding the organization's income and benefit. The presentation of momentous models, like the Model S, Model 3, Model X, and Model Y, has extended Tesla's market reach as well as situated the organization as a forerunner in the electric vehicle market.

The interest for electric vehicles, driven by expanding natural awareness, government impetuses, and progressions in battery innovation, essentially influences Tesla's monetary presentation. As buyers shift towards economical transportation choices, the deals and creation quantities of Tesla's EVs become essential signs of the organization's monetary wellbeing. Tesla's capacity to satisfy the need for its vehicles, particularly leader models like the Model 3, impacts its income streams and market capitalization.

Moreover, Tesla's prosperity is unpredictably attached to its mechanical ability. The organization's accentuation on persistent development in battery innovation, electric drivetrains, and independent dividing capacities sets it in the serious scene. Innovative headways not just upgrade the exhibition and allure of Tesla's vehicles yet in addition add to the organization's capacity to set industry principles.

The turn of events and execution of Autopilot, Tesla's high level driver-help framework, is a great representation. Autopilot's prosperity not just improves the security highlights of Tesla's vehicles yet additionally positions the organization at the very front of the race towards independent driving. The view of Tesla as an imaginative forerunner in car innovation can impact financial backer certainty, affecting the organization's stock costs and monetary standing.

Notwithstanding mechanical developments, Tesla's capacity to oversee and control creation costs is a basic consider its monetary standing. The creation productivity accomplished through the Gigafactories, especially the Gigafactory in Nevada, is intended to lessen the expense of batteries and improve generally speaking assembling capacities. Economies of scale in battery creation add to making electric vehicles more reasonable, accordingly growing Tesla's market reach.

Notwithstanding, creation challenges, as seen during the increase of the Model 3, can present dangers to Tesla's monetary steadiness. Delays, store network disturbances, and creation bottlenecks influence the organization's capacity to satisfy client need and can prompt variances in its monetary execution. Tesla's responsiveness to such difficulties, as shown during the Model 3 creation "damnation," impacts financial backer certainty and impression of the organization's functional strength.

Government strategies and motivators likewise assume a vital part in molding Tesla's monetary scene. Administrative help for electric vehicles, tax breaks, and impetuses for sustainable power arrangements influence both customer interest and the expenses related with Tesla's tasks. The accessibility of government endowments can fundamentally impact the reasonableness and allure of Tesla's items, straightforwardly influencing marketing projections and monetary results.

Then again, administrative difficulties, like changes in outflow norms or exchange arrangements, can present dangers to Tesla's monetary standing. The organization's worldwide tasks open it to assorted administrative conditions, requiring flexibility to conform to shifting guidelines. Administrative changes can influence creation costs, market access, and in general monetary execution.

Tesla's monetary standing is likewise impacted by its introduction to energy items, including sunlight based chargers and energy stockpiling arrangements. The outcome of these endeavors relies upon the more extensive market acknowledgment of environmentally friendly power arrangements and government approaches supporting the change to feasible energy. The procurement of SolarCity in 2016 denoted

Tesla's essential move into the sun powered energy area, adding to an expanded item portfolio.

In any case, the mix of SolarCity was met with debate and monetary examination. Pundits scrutinized the reasoning behind the obtaining and raised worries about expected irreconcilable situations, given Elon Musk's connections to SolarCity. The monetary presentation of Tesla's energy items, thusly, turns into a calculate molding financial backer certainty and view of the organization's essential choices.

Tesla's monetary standing is likewise dependent upon the unpredictability of monetary business sectors. As a public corporation, Tesla's stock costs are impacted by market opinion, financial backer insights, and more extensive monetary circumstances.

The organization's consideration in records like the S&P 500 has elevated its perceivability in monetary business sectors, prompting expanded examination and expected influence on its stock execution.

Additionally, Tesla's monetary standing is interlaced with the individual brand and public picture of its President, Elon Musk. Musk's flighty correspondence style, utilization of web-based entertainment, and intermittent contentions can possibly impact market insights and effect Tesla's stock costs. Musk's public assertions, for example, tweets about taking Tesla private or declarations with respect to digital money speculations, have shown the influence of his effect on Tesla's monetary scene.

The worldwide international scene additionally shapes Tesla's monetary standing, especially concerning its activities in China. The progress of the Shanghai Gigafactory and Tesla's extension in the Chinese market are impacted by political relations, exchange approaches, and international pressures. Changes in political elements can affect Tesla's admittance to key business sectors, creation expenses, and by and large monetary execution.

Tesla's monetary story is additionally affected by its essential choices with respect to capital designation. The organization's decisions connected with capital raising, obligation issuance, and interests in innovative work shape its monetary design and liquidity. Tesla's choices to give new offers, assume obligation, or send capital in regions like Gigafactories, research offices, and mechanical headways mirror its drawn out vision and impact its monetary standing.

Moreover, Tesla's monetary standing is dependent upon industry patterns and cutthroat elements. The development of new contestants in the electric vehicle market, headways by customary automakers in electric innovation, and changes in purchaser inclinations can affect Tesla's piece of the pie and monetary execution. The organization's capacity to keep an upper hand through development, marking, and creation versatility is essential in exploring the consistently developing scene of the auto business.

Ecological and social factors likewise add to the forming of Tesla's monetary account. As worldwide consciousness of environmental change develops, customer inclinations are progressively lined up with practical and harmless to the ecosystem decisions. Tesla's obligation to clean energy arrangements and its commitment to decreasing fossil fuel byproducts position the organization well in a market where ecological cognizance impacts buying choices.

7.4 The unique position of Tesla in the eyes of investors.

Tesla possesses a special and unrivaled situation according to financial backers, remaining at the crossing point of mechanical development, supportable arrangements, and the development of the auto and energy enterprises. The organization's uniqueness is established in a blend of variables that poor person just molded its monetary story however have likewise reclassified financial backer discernments and assumptions in the more extensive market.

One of the key elements adding to Tesla's remarkable position is its visionary and appealling President, Elon Musk. Musk's impact on Tesla's picture goes past customary President jobs, as he is seen as the essence of the organization as well as a main thrust behind its bold objectives and extraordinary vision. Musk's capacity to express a convincing story, combined with his eccentric correspondence style on stages like Twitter, has made an unmistakable brand character for Tesla.

Financial backers view Musk as something beyond a President; he is viewed as an innovative visionary who is pushing the limits of innovation and manageability. Musk's standing for facing challenges and rocking the boat has produced a degree of fervor and interest in the speculation local area. Notwithstanding, this flighty authority style has likewise prompted periodic contentions and elevated unpredictability in Tesla's stock cost, mirroring the remarkable elements of Musk's effect on the organization's monetary standing.

Another variable adding to Tesla's special position is its job as a trailblazer in the electric vehicle (EV) market. Tesla's initial section into the EV space, combined with its steady spotlight on pushing the limits of battery innovation and electric drivetrains, has situated the organization as an industry chief. Financial backers view Tesla as something beyond an automaker; it is viewed as a disruptor that has reclassified the potential outcomes of electric versatility.

The progress of Tesla's electric vehicles, outstandingly the Model S, Model 3, and Model Y, has exhibited the market reasonability of EVs as well as set another norm for execution, plan, and reach. Financial backers perceive Tesla's commitment to the speed increase of the worldwide change towards practical transportation, and this acknowledgment has converted into an extraordinary degree of excitement and trust in Tesla's market potential.

Tesla's novel position is additionally emphasizd by its strength in the extravagance electric vehicle market. While different automakers have entered the EV space, Tesla's capacity to consolidate extravagance with manageability has separate it. The allure of Tesla's vehicles goes past their natural certifications; they are viewed as superficial points of interest, exemplifying a pledge to development and ground breaking. This discernment has drawn in a particular fragment of shoppers, adding to Tesla's exceptional market situating.

The organization's Gigafactories assume a vital part in molding its novel standing. The Gigafactory idea addresses an essential move to coordinate creation, especially in the basic part of batteries in an upward direction. By creating batteries at scale, Tesla means to accomplish cost efficiencies and address one of the essential difficulties in the electric vehicle industry — battery costs. Financial backers perceive the meaning of Tesla's Gigafactories in driving down creation costs and supporting the organization's capacity to fulfill developing need.

The Gigafactory in Nevada, specifically, stands apart as an image of Tesla's obligation to enormous scope creation and manageability. Financial backers view these offices as assembling plants as well as essential resources that position Tesla at the front of the electric vehicle and sustainable power enterprises. The scale and desire of the Gigafactories add to Tesla's novel allure, building up the impression of the organization as a pioneer in clean energy and transportation.

Tesla's situating in the energy area is one more unmistakable perspective that catches the consideration of financial backers. The securing of SolarCity in 2016 denoted Tesla's entrance into sun powered energy and energy stockpiling arrangements. While the move was met with distrust and discussion, it mirrored Musk's vision of making an incorporated supportable energy biological system. Financial backers perceive the expected collaborations between Tesla's electric vehicles and energy items, seeing the organization as an all encompassing player in the change to a carbon-impartial future.

The monetary mix of energy items, like sunlight based chargers and Powerwall energy capacity arrangements, adds to Tesla's special allure. Financial backers see Tesla not just as an automaker but rather as a broadened energy organization with a thorough way to deal with tending to worldwide maintainability challenges. This enhancement lines up with the more extensive pattern in financial backer inclinations for organizations with an all encompassing and long haul vision for natural and social obligation.

Tesla's novel standing is additionally exemplified by its headways in independent driving innovation. The improvement of Autopilot, Tesla's high level driver-help framework, has situated the organization as a leader in the race towards completely independent vehicles. Financial backers consider Tesla to be a vehicle producer as well as an innovation organization with the possibility to rethink the fate of transportation.

The information driven way to deal with independent driving, utilizing certifiable information gathered from Tesla vehicles, separates the organization. Financial backers perceive the essential worth of Tesla's huge dataset, which is seen as an upper hand in preparing AI calculations for independent capacities. The advancement in Full Self-Driving (FSD) highlights and the commitment of over-the-air updates to upgrade vehicle capacities add to Tesla's charm as a tech-driven auto pioneer.

Moreover, Tesla's situating in the capital business sectors has added to its uniqueness. The organization's choice to open up to the world in 2010 denoted a groundbreaking second in its excursion. Tesla turned into the principal American carmaker to open up to the world since Passage in 1956, and the Initial public offering flagged a takeoff from the conventional methodology of car organizations. This move permitted Tesla to get to capital from public business sectors, powering its aggressive development designs and adding to its interesting remaining as a public disruptor.

Tesla's consideration in significant stock files, including the S&P 500, affects the more extensive venture scene. The organization's market capitalization, now and again incredible conventional automakers, mirrors the certainty and assumptions for financial backers. The sheer size of Tesla's fairly estimated worth has made it a point of convergence for conversations about market elements, valuation measurements, and the job of problematic innovations in molding the fate of money.

The remarkable place of Tesla according to financial backers is likewise impacted by its worldwide extension procedures. The launch of Gigafactories in different areas, for example, China and Germany, highlights Tesla's obligation to taking advantage of key business sectors and adjusting to provincial inclinations. Financial backers view Tesla's worldwide impression as an upper hand, permitting the organization to explore different administrative conditions, access neighborhood ability, and answer market elements with deftness.

Be that as it may, Tesla's novel position isn't without difficulties and contentions. The organization's dependence on administrative credits for income, incidental creation challenges, and the examination encompassing Musk's public explanations add to the complex account of Tesla's uniqueness. Financial backers wrestle with adjusting excitement for Tesla's problematic potential with the inborn vulnerabilities and dangers related with its offbeat methodology.

Chapter 8

The Road Ahead

The street ahead for Tesla is both energizing and testing, set apart by the proceeded with quest for development, maintainability, and market strength. As the organization explores a scene formed by quick mechanical headways, moving purchaser inclinations, and worldwide financial elements, the difficulties and open doors that lie ahead will shape Tesla's direction in the auto and energy businesses.

At the cutting edge of Tesla's process is the continuous development of electric vehicle (EV) innovation. The organization's obligation to propelling battery innovation, expanding energy thickness, and improving the productivity of electric drivetrains highlights its assurance to push the limits of what is conceivable. Tesla's interest in innovative work, combined with the essential meaning of its Gigafactories, positions the organization to stay a forerunner in the worldwide progress to electric portability.

The improvement of the Cybertruck, Tesla's all-electric pickup truck, embodies the organization's forward-looking methodology. Revealed with strong plan components and inventive highlights, the Cybertruck expects to grow Tesla's market venture into the rewarding truck portion. The progress of the Cybertruck, set to be created at the Gigafactory in Texas, will assume a significant part in deciding Tesla's capacity to take care of different customer inclinations and lay out a fortification in key market fragments.

Independent driving innovation addresses another boondocks that will shape Tesla's future. The quest for Full Self-Driving (FSD) capacities has been a point of convergence of Tesla's endeavors, with the commitment of changing individual transportation. The street ahead includes tending to specialized difficulties, administrative contemplations, and public acknowledgment of independent vehicles. Tesla's interesting methodology, utilizing genuine information from its broad armada, positions the organization at the front of the independent driving race.

The presentation of the Tesla Bot, a humanoid robot intended to perform errands and explore complex conditions, adds another aspect to the organization's introduction to mechanical technology and computerized reasoning. While the Tesla Bot is still in its calculated stage, its improvement flags Musk's vision of making flexible mechanical arrangements that can expand human abilities. The outcome of such undertakings won't just effect Tesla's item portfolio yet in addition impact the more extensive scene of robotization and advanced mechanics.

Manageability stays a center mainstay of Tesla's central goal, stretching out past electric vehicles to incorporate the whole energy environment. The extension of Tesla's energy items, including sunlight based chargers, Powerwall energy capacity arrangements, and the improvement of utility-scale projects, positions the organization as a complete player in the change to clean energy. The street ahead includes increasing energy items, expanding openness, and adding to the decarbonization of the power area.

The combination of sun powered energy and energy stockpiling arrangements picked up speed with the improvement of the Sun oriented Rooftop, an item intended to consistently incorporate sun based innovation into customary roofing materials. Tesla's capacity to make sunlight based energy tastefully engaging and financially suitable for mortgage holders is a basic consider the outcome of the Sun oriented Rooftop. As the world wrestles with the basic of economical energy arrangements, the street ahead for Tesla includes exploring the intricacies of the sustainable power market.

The international scene will likewise assume a critical part in forming Tesla's future. The organization's tasks in China, a critical market for electric vehicles, present the two open doors and difficulties. The outcome of the Shanghai Gigafactory, combined with Tesla's endeavors to confine creation and adjust to Chinese buyer inclinations, highlights the essential significance of the Chinese market. Be that as it may, exploring international strains and administrative structures will require readiness and discretion in the years to come.

Tesla's venture into other worldwide business sectors, including Europe and India, adds further layers of intricacy to its global procedure. Adjusting to different administrative conditions, tending to territorial foundation difficulties, and understanding neighborhood shopper necessities will be essential in laying out areas of strength for an in these business sectors. The street ahead includes expanding market infiltration as well as building versatile stockpile binds and answering developing international elements.

The electric vehicle market itself is going through a change, with customary automakers increasing their endeavors to rival Tesla. The street ahead includes exploring expanded contest, not just in the extravagance EV portion where Tesla has generally overwhelmed yet additionally in the mid-reach and mass-market fragments. The progress of Tesla's Model 3 in carrying electric vehicles to a more extensive purchaser base has started a trend, and the organization's capacity to remain ahead in a quickly developing business sector will be a vital determinant of its future achievement.

Charging foundation addresses a basic part of the street ahead for electric vehicles. Tesla's Supercharger network has been an upper hand, giving quick and helpful charging to Tesla proprietors. As the electric vehicle market grows, the requirement for a vigorous charging framework turns out to be more articulated. The street ahead for Tesla includes extending its Supercharger network as well as teaming up with different partners to make a normalized and interoperable charging environment.

The administrative scene will keep on impacting Tesla's activities. As state run administrations all over the planet set aggressive focuses for diminishing fossil fuel by-products and progressively transitioning away from gas powered motor vehicles, the street ahead includes lining up with advancing administrative systems. Motivations for electric vehicles, emanations norms, and strategies advancing economical transportation will shape the interest for Tesla's items and effect the organization's market situating.

Monetary contemplations will likewise assume an essential part in Tesla's excursion ahead. The organization's capacity to keep up with productivity, oversee creation versatility, and explore variances in market opinion will be vital. Tesla's monetary flexibility during testing periods, for example, the interruptions brought about by the Coronavirus pandemic, has supported financial backer certainty. The street ahead includes supporting monetary wellbeing while at the same time making vital interests in exploration, improvement, and creation limit.

The job of Tesla's Chief, Elon Musk, stays fundamental to the organization's future. Musk's authority style, unusual correspondence, and active contribution in item improvement have been characterizing attributes of Tesla's prosperity. The street ahead includes offsetting Musk's visionary initiative with corporate administration contemplations, financial backer relations, and the requests of working a worldwide undertaking. Musk's capacity to explore the intricacies of driving an organization at the front of development will be a basic consider Tesla's proceeded with progress.

As Tesla outlines its course for the future, the organization's obligation to natural supportability and clean energy arrangements will be investigated. Financial backers, shoppers, and partners progressively focus on organizations that show a certifiable obligation to tending to environmental change. The street ahead includes meeting current supportability objectives as well as setting new benchmarks and adding to worldwide endeavors to accomplish a carbon-nonpartisan future.

The cultural effect of Tesla's items and advancements will likewise shape the street ahead. As electric vehicles become more standard and independent driving innovation develops, the ramifications for metropolitan preparation, transportation foundation, and by and large portability examples will be significant. Tesla's part in affecting these progressions will stretch out past conventional auto contemplations, impacting the more extensive scene of brilliant urban communities and supportable transportation.

8.1 Future Innovations and Market Dynamics

The future for Tesla is portrayed by a steady quest for development and a unique exchange of market influences that will shape the scene of the auto and energy ventures. As the organization keeps on pushing mechanical limits, present earth shattering items, and answer developing customer assumptions, the crossing point of future advancements and market elements will be integral to Tesla's direction.

One of the critical areas of development that will characterize Tesla's future is the headway of electric vehicle (EV) innovation. The continuous innovative work endeavors zeroed in on upgrading battery execution, expanding energy thickness, and decreasing expenses are central to the organization's main goal of speeding up the world's change to reasonable energy. The advancement of cutting edge batteries, for example, strong state batteries, holds the possibility to additionally reform the EV scene by tending to go limits and charging times.

Tesla's obligation to extending its electric vehicle setup will be a main impetus in catching different market fragments. The forthcoming arrival of the Tesla Cybertruck addresses an intense introduction to the pickup truck market, consolidating the advantages of electric portability with rough utility. This move broadens Tesla's item portfolio as well as positions the organization to take advantage of the prominence of pickup trucks in business sectors like the US.

The Roadster, set to make a return with the cutting edge cycle, represents Tesla's devotion to elite execution electric vehicles. The joining of state of the art innovations, remembering progressions for optimal design and materials, will probably situate the new Roadster as a lead model displaying the zenith of Tesla's designing capacities. These developments add to Tesla's picture as an optimistic brand at the front line of auto innovation.

Independent driving innovation addresses one more outskirts of development that will shape Tesla's future. The continuous improvement of Full Self-Driving (FSD) capacities and the coordination of man-made brainpower into vehicle frameworks mark a change in perspective in the car business. Tesla's novel methodology of utilizing genuine information from its broad armada of vehicles for AI separates it from customary automakers and tech organizations.

The street ahead for independent driving includes tending to administrative difficulties, refining wellbeing highlights, and accomplishing a degree of unwavering quality that earns far reaching public acknowledgment.

As Tesla keeps on sending over-the-air updates to further develop Autopilot usefulness, the change towards full independence is supposed to be steady, with expanding levels of computerization presented over the long haul. The cultural ramifications of independent vehicles stretch out past private transportation, impacting metropolitan preparation, traffic the executives, and by and large versatility environments.

The Tesla Bot, a humanoid robot intended for universally useful undertakings, acquaints another aspect with the organization's endeavors into mechanical technology and man-made reasoning. While the advancement of the Tesla Bot is still in its beginning phases, the idea lines up with Elon Musk's vision of tending to work deficiencies and enlarging human abilities. The likely effect of Tesla's introduction to mechanical technology stretches out past auto applications, flagging a more extensive desire to add to the development of robotization.

The energy area is another field where Tesla's future developments will assume a vital part. The proceeded with improvement of energy items, including sunlight based chargers and energy stockpiling arrangements, adds to the organization's vision of making a complete maintainable energy biological system. The advancement of the Sun oriented Rooftop, intended to flawlessly incorporate sun based innovation into customary roofing materials, holds guarantee for far reaching reception by property holders looking for stylishly satisfying and energy-effective arrangements.

Tesla's energy stockpiling items, for example, the Powerwall and Powerpack, address the irregularity of environmentally friendly power sources by giving effective energy stockpiling answers for private and business applications. As the world wrestles with the basic of progressing to clean energy, Tesla's developments in energy capacity add to the dependability and versatility of sustainable power frameworks.

The improvement of utility-scale energy projects, for example, the Hornsdale Power Hold in Australia, features Tesla's ability to add to matrix solidness and backing the reconciliation of sustainable power at a huge scope. The development of such undertakings, combined with headways in matrix innovations and energy the board, positions Tesla as a vital participant in reshaping the fate of the energy business.

The mix of Tesla's electric vehicles with its energy items addresses a synergistic way to deal with supportability. The idea of vehicle-to-matrix (V2G) innovation, where electric vehicles can take care of energy back into the lattice during top interest periods, holds the possibility to change how energy is created, put away, and appropriated. This all encompassing methodology lines up with Tesla's general objective of making an interconnected biological system where transportation and energy arrangements work consistently together.

The market elements that will impact Tesla's future are intrinsically connected to more extensive patterns in the auto and energy enterprises. The worldwide change towards jolt is picking up speed, with a rising number of nations reporting intends to transition away from gas powered motor vehicles. Tesla's job in driving this progress positions the organization at the front of a change in outlook that stretches out past individual market fragments.

Government approaches and administrative systems will keep on molding the market elements for Tesla. Motivators for electric vehicles, emanations guidelines, and supportability targets will influence the interest for Tesla's items. The organization's capacity to explore and adjust to assorted administrative conditions across various districts will be pivotal in supporting business sector authority.

The serious scene is advancing quickly, with conventional automakers escalating their endeavors in the electric vehicle space. Tesla's future achievement depends on its capacity to keep an upper hand through development, creation versatility, and brand bid. The organization's lead in battery innovation, charging foundation, and programming capacities stays vital to separating itself from the opposition.

Charging foundation is a basic part of the market elements for electric vehicles. Tesla's Supercharger network has been an upper hand, giving a consistent and quick charging experience for Tesla proprietors. As the electric vehicle market extends, joint efforts and normalizations in charging foundation will turn out to be progressively significant. The interoperability of charging networks and the expansion of quick charging arrangements will impact buyer reception of electric vehicles.

Customer inclinations and assumptions will assume a significant part in molding the market elements for Tesla. As supportability mindfulness develops, purchasers are putting more noteworthy accentuation on eco-accommodating transportation arrangements. Tesla's obligation to clean energy, combined with the exhibition and plan of its vehicles, reverberates with a fragment of purchasers looking for both ecological obligation and state of the art innovation.

The moderateness of electric vehicles is a key component impacting market elements. Tesla's future achievement will include tending to the test of making electric vehicles more open to a more extensive scope of purchasers. The mass-market allure of models like the Model 3 has started a trend, and Tesla's capacity to additionally diminish costs, increment creation effectiveness, and present passage level models will be instrumental in growing its piece of the pie.

International contemplations will keep on affecting Tesla's worldwide activities. The organization's presence in key business sectors, like China, includes exploring discretionary relations, exchange arrangements, and international pressures. The street ahead for Tesla in developing business sectors, including India, will require key transformations to nearby circumstances and inclinations.

Monetary contemplations will stay a key part of Tesla's excursion. The organization's capacity to support productivity, oversee capital assignment, and asset continuous innovative work drives will be pivotal. Tesla's consideration in significant stock lists and its market capitalization will keep on reflecting financial backer certainty, and the organization's monetary flexibility during monetary vulnerabilities will be firmly observed.

The cultural effect of Tesla's developments will stretch out past the prompt business sectors for electric vehicles and clean energy. As Tesla's advances impact transportation, energy, and computerization, the organization's job in forming the eventual fate of savvy urban areas, reasonable foundation, and worldwide endeavors to battle environmental change will be huge. The cultural advantages of lessening fossil fuel byproducts, further developing energy productivity, and upgrading by and large personal satisfaction add to the more extensive story of Tesla's effect.

8.2 Speculations on upcoming innovations.

As Tesla keeps on driving the charge in the car and energy areas, hypotheses about impending advancements proliferate, energized by the organization's set of experiences of pushing mechanical limits and reclassifying industry principles. While exact subtleties of Tesla's future advancements remain strictly confidential, there are a few regions where industry spectators, devotees, and examiners are estimating on what may be coming up for the electric vehicle (EV) trailblazer.

**1. ** Cutting edge Battery Innovation:

One of the most expected areas of advancement for Tesla is the improvement of cutting edge battery innovation. The journey for higher energy thickness, longer reach, and quicker charging times has been a main impetus for Tesla's innovative work endeavors. Hypotheses recommend that Tesla could be dealing with strong state batteries, which can possibly offer critical enhancements over current lithium-particle innovation. Strong state batteries guarantee expanded energy thickness, upgraded wellbeing, and quicker charging, tending to a portion of the critical difficulties in electric vehicle reception.

The improvement of cutting edge battery innovation isn't just significant for electric vehicles yet in addition assumes a vital part in Tesla's energy stockpiling arrangements. Enhancements in energy thickness could prompt more minimal and productive home energy stockpiling units, further supporting Tesla's situation in the sustainable power biological system.

2. Vehicle-to-Matrix (V2G) Joining:

One more area of hypothesis rotates around the joining of Vehicle-to-Matrix (V2G) innovation in Tesla's electric vehicles. V2G innovation empowers bidirectional energy stream between electric vehicles and the matrix, permitting vehicles to draw power as well as feed abundance energy back into the network. This can possibly transform Tesla's armada of vehicles into a disseminated energy asset, adding to network security and versatility.

Hypotheses propose that Tesla could use its high level battery innovation and programming abilities to empower V2G usefulness. This advancement could change Tesla vehicles into versatile power sources, especially during top interest periods or in regions with irregular sustainable power age. The coordination of V2G innovation lines up with Tesla's comprehensive way to deal with economical energy arrangements.

3. Headways in Autopilot and Full Self-Driving (FSD):

The development of independent driving innovation is a constant concentration for Tesla, and hypotheses flourish in regards to progressions in the Autopilot and Full Self-Driving (FSD) capacities. Tesla's armada of vehicles furnished with cutting edge driver-help frameworks ceaselessly gathers information, adding to the AI calculations that power independent driving highlights.

Hypotheses incorporate the rollout of more refined FSD highlights, upgraded object acknowledgment abilities, and enhancements in exploring complex metropolitan conditions. The chance of accomplishing more significant levels of independence, moving toward a completely self-driving capacity in specific situations, is a subject of hypothesis and expectation. As administrative structures develop, Tesla is supposed to use its amassed information to remain at the cutting edge of independent driving innovation.

4. Development of Energy Items:

Tesla's introduction to the energy area is probably going to see further development with better than ever energy items. Hypotheses remember progressions for sunlight based charger innovation, making sun powered energy more productive and practical. The Sun powered Rooftop, intended to consistently incorporate sun oriented innovation into customary roofing materials, could see boundless reception as Tesla refines and extends its contributions.

In addition, hypotheses encompass the advancement of cutting edge energy capacity arrangements. Tesla's Powerwall and Powerpack have shown the worth of home and business energy capacity, and future developments might include expanded capacity limit, further developed proficiency, and new applications for energy capacity frameworks.

5. Passage into New Vehicle Fragments:

While Tesla has had a tremendous effect in the extravagance and mass-market electric vehicle fragments, there are hypotheses about the organization entering new vehicle portions. The uncovering of the Tesla Cybertruck flagged the organization's expectation to contend in the pickup truck market. Hypotheses presently center around likely sections into different portions, for example, smaller vehicles or even electric vans, extending Tesla's market reach.

Tesla's capacity to offer electric vehicles at various price tags and for different use cases could be an essential move to catch a more extensive piece of the pie. The interest for electric vehicles is developing, and entering new fragments would line up with Tesla's main goal of speeding up the change to reasonable transportation.

6. Gigafactory Developments:

Tesla's Gigafactories are key to its system of accomplishing economies of scale underway. Hypotheses encompass the chance of new Gigafactory areas and extensions of existing offices. As Tesla means to fulfill expanding need for its vehicles and energy items, extra Gigafactories could be laid out in districts with high market potential.

Developments could likewise include the coordination of new advances and creation processes. The Gigafactory in Texas, for instance, is supposed to highlight developments in assembling, and comparable headways could be integrated into future Gigafactory projects.

7. Expanded Reality (AR) for Vehicle Upkeep:

There are theories about Tesla utilizing increased reality (AR) for vehicle upkeep and overhauling. AR innovation could be utilized to give continuous, intelligent direction to Tesla proprietors for routine upkeep assignments, investigating, and minor fixes. This could improve the general possession experience by enabling clients to perform essential support assignments with direction from the Tesla application.

By coordinating AR into the help insight, Tesla could smooth out the support cycle, lessen the requirement for actual help community visits, and give a more easy to understand interface for vehicle proprietors. This speculative development lines up with Tesla's accentuation on state of the art innovation and client driven plan.

8. Reasonable Materials and Assembling:

As manageability turns into an undeniably significant thought in the auto business, hypotheses center around Tesla's endeavors to integrate more maintainable materials into its vehicles and upgrade producing processes for ecological effect. This could include the utilization of reused materials, eco-accommodating assembling rehearses, and a proceeded with obligation to lessening the carbon impression of Tesla's tasks.

The quest for maintainability reaches out past the actual vehicles to the whole inventory network and creation cycle. Tesla's emphasis on limiting ecological effect lines up with more extensive industry patterns and purchaser assumptions for naturally cognizant assembling rehearses.

9. Tesla's Job in Brilliant Urban communities:

Hypotheses additionally stretch out to Tesla's expected job in molding the improvement of shrewd urban areas. As urban areas all over the planet investigate inventive answers for metropolitan preparation, transportation, and energy the board, Tesla's innovations could assume a urgent part. This incorporates the mix of Tesla vehicles into savvy city organizations, improved traffic the executives through independent driving abilities, and cooperative endeavors to establish supportable metropolitan conditions.

The interconnectedness of Tesla's electric vehicles, energy items, and expected commitments to brilliant city drives could situate the organization as a vital participant in the more extensive change of metropolitan living.

10. Joint effort with Different Enterprises:

There are theories about Tesla investigating joint efforts with different enterprises beyond car and energy. As the lines between innovation, transportation, and different areas obscure, Tesla's mastery in electric vehicles, batteries, and programming could track down applications past customary limits.

Potential joint efforts could include associations with innovation organizations, foundation suppliers, or even medical care associations. The combination of Tesla's advances into different ventures could open up new roads for development and add to the organization's development and impact.

8.3 Anticipation of market dynamics in the electric vehicle industry.

The electric vehicle (EV) industry is at a vital point, with quick headways in innovation, moving purchaser inclinations, and worldwide endeavors to address environmental change driving exceptional development and development. As the electric vehicle market keeps on developing, there is an uplifted expectation of massive changes in market elements that will shape the business' direction before very long.

**1. ** Growing Item Contributions and Market Division:

One of the critical expectations in the electric vehicle industry is the development of item contributions and expanded market division. Generally, electric vehicles were related with top of the line, extravagance models. Nonetheless, there is a developing assumption that automakers will expand their electric vehicle portfolios to take care of a more extensive scope of customers.

Significant automakers, enlivened by the outcome of Tesla's Model 3, are supposed to acquaint more reasonable electric models with enter the mass market. This shift is expected to speed up the reception of electric vehicles among a more extensive shopper base, making reasonable transportation more open and interesting to the typical buyer.

The rising business sector division additionally incorporates the expected passage of electric vehicles into new portions, for example, pickup trucks and SUVs. The outcome of electric models in these famous vehicle classes could additionally set the place of electric vehicles in the standard auto market.

**2. ** Advancing Charging Framework:

Expectation encompasses the development of charging framework as a basic variable impacting the electric vehicle market. The development of the electric vehicle market is dependent upon the accessibility of a hearty and boundless charging organization. Partners, including automakers, states, and confidential substances, are expected to put fundamentally in extending and upgrading charging foundation.

The advancement of quicker charging innovations and the multiplication of charging stations in metropolitan regions, along thruways, and at working environments are normal. This expectation is energized by the acknowledgment that tending to "range uneasiness" — the feeling of dread toward running out of battery power prior to arriving at a charging station — is urgent in empowering more extensive electric vehicle reception.

Also, industry players are investigating developments in charging innovation, including remote charging and super quick charging arrangements, to make the charging experience more advantageous and effective. The expectation is that headways in charging foundation will add to the consistent mix of electric vehicles into day to day existence.

**3. ** Government Motivating forces and Guidelines:

Expectation likewise spins around the job of government motivating forces and guidelines in forming the electric vehicle market. States overall are progressively perceiving the ecological advantages of electric vehicles and are supposed to acquaint or upgrade motivators with support their reception.

These motivations might incorporate tax reductions, discounts, and endowments for the two shoppers and producers. Also, stricter outflows principles and guidelines inclining toward electric vehicles over conventional gas powered motor vehicles are expected. The arrangement of government strategies with the advancement of maintainable transportation is supposed to significantly affect the electric vehicle market elements.

Expected administrative apportions incorporate the staging of petroleum derivative controlled vehicles, the foundation of zero-emanation zones in metropolitan regions, and the burden of tough discharge principles. The proactive position of state run administrations in supporting electric portability is probably going to speed up the progress toward cleaner transportation choices.

**4. ** Mechanical Advancements and Reach Improvement:

The expectation of consistent mechanical developments is a main thrust in the electric vehicle industry. One of the determined difficulties for electric vehicles has been tending to worries about range limits. Industry partners are effectively chipping away at headways in battery innovation to increment energy thickness, upgrade charging speed, and further develop generally battery execution.

The expectation is that forward leaps in battery innovation, for example, the advancement of strong state batteries, will prompt electric vehicles with fundamentally expanded ranges. This, thus, is supposed to take out range nervousness and make electric vehicles a more alluring choice for shoppers with longer driving distances.

Moreover, mechanical advancements stretch out to upgrades in electric drivetrains, lightweight materials, and streamlined features, adding to expanded energy proficiency and improved generally speaking vehicle execution. As electric vehicle innovation develops, expectations incorporate more modern energy the board frameworks and the coordination of man-made consciousness for streamlining battery use.

**5. ** Worldwide Development and Market Infiltration:

Expectations likewise base on the worldwide extension of electric vehicle producers and expanded market entrance in locales past conventional fortifications. The push for maintainable transportation is turning into a worldwide peculiarity, with different nations focusing on progressively eliminating gas powered motor vehicles in the next few decades.

Significant automakers and electric vehicle new businesses are supposed to zero in on extending their market presence in districts with high development potential, including Asia, Europe, and developing business sectors. Expected procedures include adjusting items to neighborhood inclinations, laying out organizations with nearby elements, and exploring administrative scenes novel to every locale.

Besides, the expectation is that global joint effort and the sharing of mechanical aptitude will turn out to be more predominant in the electric vehicle industry. Crossline organizations and joint endeavors could work with the trading of information and assets, encouraging a more interconnected and cooperative way to deal with tending to worldwide transportation challenges.

**6. ** Purchaser Mindfulness and Schooling:

As electric vehicles become more standard, there is a developing expectation of expanded purchaser mindfulness and schooling about the advantages of electric portability. The outcome of electric vehicles depends on customers settling on informed decisions in view of a comprehension of the innovation, natural effect, and long haul cost reserve funds.

Expected endeavors incorporate thorough advertising efforts via automakers, government drives to teach the general population, and cooperation between industry partners to scatter fantasies and misinterpretations about electric vehicles. Customer schooling is urgent for scattering legends connected with range tension, charging foundation, and the general common sense of electric vehicles for regular use.

**7. ** Mix of Environmentally friendly power Sources:

The expectation stretches out to the reconciliation of sustainable power sources to drive electric vehicles. With a developing accentuation on manageability, there is an assumption that electric vehicle proprietors will progressively try to charge their vehicles utilizing environmentally friendly power, for example, sunlight based or wind power.

The combination of home sun powered chargers with electric vehicle charging stations is an expected pattern, permitting customers to create their own perfect energy for transportation.

Moreover, coordinated efforts between electric utilities and electric vehicle producers are supposed to advance the utilization of sustainable power for charging at public charging stations.

**8. ** Rivalry and Market Union:

Expectations additionally revolve around the heightening of contest and potential market union in the electric vehicle industry. As additional automakers enter the electric vehicle market and conventional producers progress to electric models, there is an expectation of expanded rivalry for piece of the pie.

This elevated rivalry is supposed to drive development, lower costs, and extend purchaser decisions. All the while, there is an expectation of likely consolidations, acquisitions, and key partnerships as organizations look to reinforce their situations in the advancing business sector. The rise of predominant players and the combination of piece of the pie are expected results of this cutthroat scene.

8.4 Consideration of potential challenges and opportunities.

The electric vehicle (EV) industry, while encountering critical development and advancement, isn't without its difficulties and potential open doors. As the world turns towards feasible transportation, there are contemplations that length innovative, financial, administrative, and cultural aspects. In exploring these intricacies, industry partners should be aware of expected moves while utilizing chances to additionally speed up the change to electric portability.

**1. ** Difficulties in Battery Innovation:

An essential test confronting the electric vehicle industry lies in the space of battery innovation. Notwithstanding progressions, concerns like restricted energy thickness, corruption over the long run, and the natural effect of battery creation continue.

The mining and extraction of unrefined components for batteries, including lithium, cobalt, and nickel, bring up moral and natural issues.

Also, the production network weakness related with these materials presents difficulties for makers. The business is effectively investigating options, for example, strong state batteries and maintainable obtaining rehearses, to address these worries. In any case, until these options are generally taken on, dealing with the ecological and social effect of battery creation stays a basic test.

**2. ** Charging Framework:

While there is a developing accentuation on extending charging foundation, the test of building a complete and easy to understand network endures. The pace of charging, normalization of charging connectors, and the openness of charging stations in provincial or less created regions are progressing difficulties. The expectation of a flood in electric vehicle reception requires a proactive way to deal with building a vigorous charging foundation that tends to these worries.

Open doors in this space incorporate coordinated effort between states, confidential elements, and automakers to put resources into charging foundation. The improvement of quicker charging advancements, savvy charging arrangements, and expanded joining with sustainable power sources address roads for defeating these difficulties.

**3. ** Reasonableness and Market Access:

The forthright expense of electric vehicles, notwithstanding diminishing over the long run, stays an obstacle for far reaching reception. The higher introductory expense contrasted with customary gas powered motor vehicles is a thought for the majority possible purchasers. While the complete expense of proprietorship, taking into account lower working and upkeep costs, is good for electric vehicles, the underlying venture can be an obstruction.

Valuable open doors lie in drives to make electric vehicles more reasonable, for example, government motivations, tax breaks, and appropriations. Expanded creation volumes and economies of scale are supposed to add to cost decreases. Market access can likewise be extended through funding choices, renting programs, and imaginative plans of action that make electric vehicles more open to a more extensive scope of purchasers.

**4. ** Buyer Mindfulness and Schooling:

A test that perseveres in the electric vehicle industry is the requirement for broad shopper mindfulness and training. Legends and confusions encompassing electric vehicles, like worries about range, charging foundation, and battery duration, add to reluctance among possible purchasers.

Potential open doors in such manner incorporate extensive showcasing and instructive missions by industry players. Cooperative endeavors between state run administrations, automakers, and promotion gatherings can scatter fantasies and give precise data to general society. As customers become more educated about the advantages regarding electric vehicles, the market is probably going to observe expanded acknowledgment and reception.

**5. ** Administrative Scene:

While legislatures all over the planet are progressively steady of electric portability, the administrative scene stays dynamic and postures the two difficulties and valuable open doors. Expected difficulties incorporate the requirement for predictable and normalized guidelines across locales, guaranteeing a level battleground for electric vehicles, and resolving issues connected with tax collection and foundation improvement.

Open doors arise through proactive coordinated effort among states and industry partners to establish a strong administrative climate. This incorporates boosting electric vehicle reception, setting discharge guidelines that favor clean transportation, and encouraging global collaboration to address administrative difficulties across borders.

**6. ** Creation Adaptability:

As interest for electric vehicles develops, guaranteeing the versatility of creation to meet market necessities turns into a thought. Challenges incorporate getting a steady store network for basic parts, like batteries, and tending to possible bottlenecks underway limit.

Open doors exist in interests in assembling abilities, key associations, and progressions underway proficiency. As electric vehicle makers increase their activities, the business can profit from economies of scale, prompting cost decreases and expanded openness for buyers.

**7. ** Mechanical Advancement and Reconciliation:

While mechanical development drives the electric vehicle industry, the test lies in really coordinating these advancements into a consistent and easy to use insight. Issues, for example, interoperability of charging foundation, programming updates, and normalization of innovations across various makers need consideration.

Open doors arise through cooperative industry drives to lay out normal principles. Open-source stages and shared mechanical systems can work with interoperability, considering a more strong electric vehicle environment. Key organizations among automakers and innovation organizations can drive development while guaranteeing similarity and usability for buyers.

**8. ** Framework Limit and Energy Supply:

The inescapable reception of electric vehicles delivers difficulties connected with the limit of electrical matrices and the general energy supply. Concentrated charging requests, particularly during busy times, can strain existing matrix foundation. Guaranteeing a solid and maintainable energy supply to fulfill the expanded need from electric vehicles is a thought for industry partners.

Amazing open doors lie in the reconciliation of shrewd lattice advancements, energy capacity arrangements, and coordination between electric utilities and charging framework suppliers. This can empower streamlined charging plans, load adjusting, and the joining of environmentally friendly power sources to moderate the effect on lattice limit.

**9. ** Second-Life Battery Use:

As electric vehicle batteries arrive at the finish of their auto life, the subject of how to reuse or reuse these batteries becomes essential. Dealing with the natural effect of end-of-life batteries and finding monetarily feasible second-life applications present difficulties for the business.

Amazing open doors incorporate the investigation of creative approaches to reuse involved batteries for energy capacity in fixed applications. This could include incorporating resigned electric vehicle batteries into framework capacity frameworks or involving them for private and business energy capacity arrangements. Vital organizations between automakers, energy organizations, and reusing offices can add to feasible battery lifecycle the executives.

**10. ** Worldwide Monetary Variables:

Financial variables, including fluctuating ware costs, international contemplations, and the general wellbeing of the worldwide economy, present difficulties for the electric vehicle industry. The production network weakness to international strains, for instance, can influence the accessibility and cost of fundamental materials.

Open doors incorporate differentiating supply chains, putting resources into home-grown creation capacities, and adjusting to advancing financial circumstances. As the business develops, vital prescience and dexterity in answering financial difficulties will be significant for supported development.

Chapter 9

A Sustainable Tomorrow

In the steadily developing embroidery of human progress, the idea of supportability has arisen as a core value for molding an agreeable concurrence among mankind and the planet. As we stand at the intersection of ecological emergencies and cultural difficulties, the basic to fashion a reasonable tomorrow has never been seriously squeezing. This excursion towards supportability envelops a complex methodology that entwines environmental equilibrium, social value, and monetary strength.

At the core of the maintainable transformation lies the affirmation of the limited idea of Earth's assets. The twentieth century saw extraordinary headways in innovation, industry, and farming, driving humankind into a period of uncommon advancement. In any case, this quick climb likewise carried with it a clouded side - ecological corruption, asset consumption, and environmental change. The acknowledgment unfolded that the common direction was impractical, provoking a change in outlook by they way we see and cooperate with our current circumstance.

The quest for maintainability requires a significant reconsideration of our relationship with nature. It requests that we rise above the extractive mentality that described a significant part of the modern age, seeing the climate not as an endless wellspring of unrefined components but rather as a sensitive trap of interconnected biological systems. In this specific situation, the protection of biodiversity arises as a key part for manageability. The unpredictable embroidery of life on The planet, from the littlest microorganisms to the biggest vertebrates, assumes a significant part in keeping up with environment strength.

Safeguarding biodiversity isn't only an ecological concern; it involves endurance for the human species. Biological systems furnish us with a horde of administrations, frequently alluded to as environment administrations, including clean air and water, fertilization of harvests, and guideline of environment. As we witness the disturbing decay of species and territories, the earnestness to protect biodiversity becomes central. Protection endeavors, upheld by global coordinated effort and local area commitment, become fundamental points of support in the development of a reasonable tomorrow.

All the while, tending to environmental change arises as a critical part of the supportability plan. The consuming of petroleum derivatives, deforestation, and modern exercises have fundamentally raised ozone depleting substance fixations in the air, prompting an Earth-wide temperature boost and erratic environment designs. The results are obvious - rising ocean levels, outrageous climate occasions, and disturbances to biological systems. To get a maintainable future, a deliberate worldwide work to progress towards sustainable power sources, upgrade energy productivity, and moderate fossil fuel byproducts is basic.

Progressing to a practical energy worldview isn't just an ecological need yet in addition an impetus for financial change. The 21st century has seen a flood in environmentally friendly power advancements, from sun based and wind to geothermal and hydropower. These innovations not just deal a cleaner option in contrast to customary petroleum derivatives yet in addition present open doors for work creation and financial development. Embracing supportable energy isn't simply an environmental basic however an essential interest in a tough and prosperous future.

Be that as it may, the excursion towards manageability reaches out past natural stewardship. Social value and equity are basic aspects that should be woven into the texture of a supportable tomorrow. The abberations that penetrate social orders around the world - be it in admittance to training, medical services, or financial open doors - are intrinsically impractical. A really feasible future requests the destroying of fundamental disparities and the development of comprehensive social orders where each individual has the potential chance to flourish.

Chasing social manageability, orientation fairness assumes a urgent part. Engaging ladies and guaranteeing their equivalent support in all features of society isn't just a question of equity however an essential basic for manageable turn of events. Ladies, especially in agricultural nations, endure the worst part of natural and social difficulties. By engaging ladies financially, socially, and strategically, social orders can bridle the maximum capacity of their human resources and encourage an additional practical and strong future.

Additionally, native information and customary practices offer important experiences for supportable living. Native people group have, for quite a long time, kept a harmonious relationship with nature, depending on customary thinking to explore their connections with the climate.

Perceiving and regarding native privileges, cultivating social variety, and coordinating customary information into current manageability endeavors are pivotal strides towards a more comprehensive and comprehensive way to deal with supportable turn of events.

Monetary manageability finishes the group of three of interconnected support points that help a reasonable tomorrow. The predominant model of constant monetary development, frequently to the detriment of natural and social contemplations, is impractical over the long haul. A change in perspective towards a round economy, where assets are utilized proficiently, squander is limited, and the ecological effect is decreased, becomes basic.

Round economies focus on the regenerative limit of normal frameworks, expecting to decouple monetary development from asset consumption. This shift requires inventive plans of action, item plan, and utilization designs that focus on life span, recyclability, and natural obligation. Embracing roundabout standards mitigates ecological debasement as well as encourages financial versatility by lessening reliance on limited assets and limiting waste.

The job of innovation in cultivating supportability couldn't possibly be more significant. The 21st century has seen a blast of innovative progressions that can possibly change how we approach ecological and social difficulties. From man-made consciousness and huge information examination to blockchain and the Web of Things, innovation offers instruments to screen, make due, and advance our communications with the climate.

Brilliant urban communities, empowered by innovation, can upgrade metropolitan manageability by enhancing asset use, further developing energy proficiency, and diminishing ecological effect. Accuracy agribusiness, worked with by sensors and information examination, can alter food creation, limiting waste and natural effect. Mechanical development, nonetheless, should be joined by moral contemplations, guaranteeing that it adds to supportability without compounding social imbalances or ecological mischief.

Schooling arises as a foundation for building a feasible tomorrow. A worldwide shift towards supportable practices requires a populace that is educated, connected with, and enabled to settle on cognizant decisions. Practical improvement objectives, woven into instructive educational programs at all levels, can develop an age that figures out the interconnections between ecological, social, and financial frameworks.

Past proper training, public mindfulness missions, and local area commitment drives assume a urgent part in encouraging a culture of supportability. People, people group, organizations, and states all play a part to play in this aggregate undertaking. The force of aggregate activity becomes apparent in developments upholding for natural preservation, environment activity, and civil rights. Grassroots drives and worldwide joint efforts the same highlight the interconnectedness of humankind and the common obligation regarding building a reasonable future.

9.1 Reflection on Tesla's role in shaping a sustainable future.

As we stand at the edge of a vital time in mankind's set of experiences, portrayed by remarkable natural difficulties and the basic to reshape our relationship with the planet, the job of creative organizations in driving manageable arrangements turns out to be progressively critical. Among these pioneers, Tesla, Inc. has arisen as a groundbreaking power, in the auto business as well as in the more extensive scene of feasible innovation. A reflection on Tesla's job in molding a manageable future uncovers a story that stretches out past electric vehicles, digging into environmentally friendly power, energy capacity, and the interconnected domains of innovation and supportability.

Tesla's process can be followed back to its establishing in 2003 by Martin Eberhard and Marc Tarpenning. In any case, it was Elon Musk, who joined as a financial backer and executive of the board in 2004, that moved Tesla into the worldwide spotlight. Musk's vision for a reasonable future, combined with his aggressive objectives and enterprising soul, has been a main impetus behind Tesla's direction. At the core of Tesla's central goal is the obligation to speeding up the world's change to feasible energy - a grand objective that rises above the limits of customary auto organizations.

The foundation of Tesla's effect on manageability lies in its spearheading endeavors to promote electric vehicles (EVs). The car business, generally dependent on non-renewable energy sources, remained at a junction as worries over environmental change and air contamination acquired unmistakable quality. Tesla's presentation of the Roadster in 2008 denoted a change in perspective, demonstrating that electric vehicles could be superior execution, sharp, and attractive. The resulting send off of the Model S in 2012 showed the way that electric vehicles could contend with, and even outperform, their inner burning partners regarding reach, speed increase, and by and large execution.

Tesla's outcome in the electric vehicle market reached out basically impossible for its to fabricate alluring vehicles. The organization decisively situated itself as a disruptor in an industry hesitant to change. The Supercharger organization, Tesla's restrictive quick charging foundation, tended to one of the key worries related with EV reception - range uneasiness. By putting resources into a vigorous charging foundation, Tesla lightened customer misgivings as well as assumed an essential part in normalizing the possibility of electric vehicles as a reasonable and helpful method of transportation.

The effect of Tesla's introduction to electric vehicles resonated a long ways past its own portion of the overall industry. Customary automakers, prodded by Tesla's prosperity, started putting vigorously in electric vehicle innovation. The opposition that resulted extended customer decisions as well as sped up mechanical headways in battery innovation, range, and charging framework. Tesla's eagerness to share its electric vehicle licenses with the business further highlighted a pledge to cooperative advancement towards a practical car scene.

In any case, Tesla's vision expands well past the streets. At the center of Elon Musk's end-all strategy for Tesla, enunciated in 2006, is an all encompassing way to deal with supportability. The arrangement envelops not just the improvement of a large number of electric vehicles yet additionally the incorporation of sun powered energy and energy stockpiling arrangements. In 2016, Tesla made a critical stride towards this vision with the obtaining of SolarCity, a sun powered energy administrations organization established by Musk's cousins. This essential move situated Tesla as a complete clean energy organization, offering arrangements that traversed transportation, energy age, and capacity.

The joining of sun powered energy into Tesla's portfolio appeared as sun oriented rooftop tiles and sunlight powered chargers. The Sun based Rooftop, uncovered in 2016, planned to reform the private sun powered market by joining energy age with stylishly satisfying roofing materials. While the reception of sun powered rooftop innovation has been steady, it connotes Tesla's obligation to enhancing across areas to address the more extensive test of progressing to feasible energy sources.

Lined up with its sun based drives, Tesla wandered into the domain of energy stockpiling with the Powerwall, Powerpack, and Megapack. These energy stockpiling arrangements are intended to outfit and store energy created from sustainable sources, giving a solid and versatile method for overseeing energy interest. The Powerwall, designated at private use, permits mortgage holders to store overabundance energy for use during times of appeal or when the sun isn't sparkling. The Powerpack and Megapack, then again, take special care of bigger scope applications, like business and utility-scale energy capacity.

The meaning of Tesla's energy stockpiling arrangements reaches out past individual buyers or organizations. By making versatile energy stockpiling frameworks, Tesla adds to the security and dependability of sustainable power sources. The irregularity of sunlight based and wind power has for quite some time been really difficult for boundless reception. Tesla's energy stockpiling arrangements offer a method for putting away overabundance energy during top age periods and delivery it when request is high or during times of low environmentally friendly power creation. This improves network flexibility as well as speeds up the progress towards a more decentralized and feasible energy framework.

A basic part of Tesla's effect on manageability lies in its accentuation on vertical coordination and development in battery innovation. The battery pack is a critical part of electric vehicles and energy stockpiling frameworks, impacting variables like reach, charging rate, and generally execution. Tesla's Gigafactories, decisively situated across the globe, are monster offices committed to the development of batteries and electric drivetrains. The Gigafactory idea addresses a takeoff from the conventional car fabricating model, underlining economies of scale and in-house creation of key parts.

Tesla's determined quest for mechanical advancement in battery innovation is exemplified by the improvement of the "4680" battery cell. Uncovered in 2020 during Tesla's Battery Day occasion, the 4680 cell addresses a critical jump forward in energy thickness, cost decrease, and assembling effectiveness. By expanding the size of the battery cell and upgrading its plan, Tesla means to improve the presentation and moderateness of its electric vehicles while additional propelling the feasibility of environmentally friendly power stockpiling arrangements.

Past its substantial items, Tesla's effect on maintainability is interwoven with its impact on the more extensive car industry and public insight. The organization's prosperity has started a worldwide change in shopper inclinations, testing the tried and true way of thinking that leaned toward gas powered motor vehicles. The optimistic allure of Tesla's electric vehicles, combined with their superior exhibition and state of the art innovation, has added to the standardization of electric vehicles as images of status, advancement, and ecological cognizance.

Tesla's impact isn't restricted to the buyer market; it reaches out to administrative and strategy areas. The progress of electric vehicles, moved by organizations like Tesla, has provoked legislatures all over the planet to authorize arrangements that boost the reception of clean energy arrangements. Endowments, tax breaks, and outflows guidelines have been made to urge buyers and organizations to embrace electric vehicles and environmentally friendly power innovations. Tesla's capacity to show the reasonability of electric vehicles as a standard choice plays had a critical impact in forming these strategy scenes.

In any case, Tesla's process has not been without difficulties and debates. The organization's forceful development targets, creation difficulties, and Musk's unfiltered correspondence style have drawn in examination. Work rehearses at Tesla's production lines, worries over work environment wellbeing, and claims of association busting have brought up moral issues about the organization's activities. Moreover, the unpredictability of Tesla's stock, powered by hypothesis and market opinion, has added a layer of intricacy to its story.

Tesla's introduction to the Chinese market likewise highlights the intricacies of working in a globalized world. While the organization has encountered critical outcome in China, turning into a central part on the planet's biggest car market, it has explored issues going from exchange pressures to quality control difficulties. The worldwide idea of Tesla's tasks features the unpredictable transaction between financial, political, and social factors that shape the scene for economical innovation organizations.

9.2 The ongoing transformation driven by Tesla's commitment.

The continuous change moved by Tesla's enduring obligation to supportability is a demonstration of the significant impact a solitary organization can apply on worldwide businesses and cultural viewpoints. At the core of this change lies Tesla's nervy mission: to speed up the world's progress to supportable energy. This mission stretches out a long ways past the domain of electric vehicles, saturating into environmentally friendly power, energy capacity, and reshaping the actual texture of how we imagine a supportable future.

Tesla's effect on the car business is permanent. The organization's persevering quest for development in electric vehicle innovation has re-imagined the potential outcomes of economical transportation as well as constrained customary automakers to recalibrate their techniques. The presentation of the Tesla Roadster in 2008 denoted a change in perspective, demonstrating that electric vehicles could be smooth, elite execution, and attractive. The resulting Model S, Model 3, Model X, and Model Y extended Tesla's arrive at across different market fragments, showing the way that electric vehicles could contend on ecological grounds as well as on execution, reach, and style.

What separates Tesla isn't simply the nature of its electric vehicles however the all encompassing methodology it takes toward manageability. The Supercharger organization, a restrictive quick charging framework, addresses a basic worry that has long prevented the far and wide reception of electric vehicles - range uneasiness. By decisively conveying Supercharger stations worldwide, Tesla has lightened customer fears as well as assumed a critical part in normalizing electric vehicles as a functional and helpful method of transportation.

Notwithstanding, Tesla's responsibility reaches out past upsetting individual transportation. The procurement of SolarCity in 2016 denoted an essential move into the domain of sun oriented energy. Elon Musk's vision for a far reaching clean energy organization started to emerge as Tesla incorporated sun powered arrangements into its portfolio. The Sun powered Rooftop, a mix of energy-creating sun oriented tiles and tastefully satisfying roofing materials, intended to reclassify private sun based innovation. While the reception of sun oriented rooftop innovation has been steady, it represents Tesla's commitment to advancing across areas to address the more extensive test of changing to practical energy sources.

Energy capacity is one more mainstay of Tesla's maintainability methodology. The Powerwall, Powerpack, and Megapack are energy stockpiling arrangements intended to supplement sustainable power sources by putting away abundance energy for use during times of appeal or when inexhaustible creation is low. These capacity arrangements improve matrix flexibility as well as assume a critical part in decoupling energy creation from petroleum derivatives. By saddling the force of batteries, Tesla adds to the improvement of a more decentralized and supportable energy foundation.

Key to Tesla's extraordinary excursion is its accentuation on vertical coordination. The Gigafactories, decisively situated across the globe, address a takeoff from customary assembling models. These giant offices are devoted to the in-house creation of batteries and electric drivetrains. The Gigafactory idea permits Tesla to accomplish economies of scale, smooth out creation processes, and apply more prominent command over the quality and cost of key parts. This upward incorporation is essential for Tesla's aggressive objectives of expanding creation limit, driving down costs, and propelling battery innovation.

A crucial second in Tesla's quest for economical energy happened with the presentation of the "4680" battery cell. Revealed during Tesla's Battery Day occasion in 2020, the 4680 cell addresses a jump forward in energy thickness and assembling proficiency. By expanding the size of the battery cell and streamlining its plan, Tesla means to upgrade the presentation and moderateness of its electric vehicles while additional propelling the feasibility of sustainable power stockpiling arrangements. This obligation to pushing the limits of battery innovation highlights Tesla's job as a driver of development in the mission for a maintainable future.

Tesla's impact broadens well past the unmistakable items it produces. The organization has turned into an image of development, pushing the limits of what is conceivable in the convergence of innovation and supportability. The optimistic allure of Tesla's electric vehicles, combined with their superior presentation and state of the art innovation, plays had a significant impact in molding buyer discernments. Electric vehicles are not generally seen as compromise arrangements however as images of status, development, and natural awareness.

Besides, Tesla's prosperity has catalyzed a worldwide change in shopper inclinations and industry elements. Customary automakers, at first wary about putting resources into electric vehicle innovation, have been compelled to reexamine their procedures right after Tesla's prosperity. The opposition that resulted has sped up headways in battery innovation, range, and charging framework, helping shoppers and driving the whole auto industry towards a more practical future.

Tesla's effect isn't restricted to the car area; it stretches out into the domain of public strategy and worldwide drives. The outcome of electric vehicles, driven to some degree by Tesla's impact, has provoked states overall to establish strategies that boost the reception of clean energy arrangements. Sponsorships, tax breaks, and emanations guidelines have been created to urge buyers and organizations to embrace electric vehicles and sustainable power innovations. Tesla's capacity to exhibit the feasibility of electric vehicles as a standard choice plays had a critical impact in molding these strategy scenes.

Nonetheless, Tesla's groundbreaking process has not been without its portion of difficulties and discussions. The organization's aggressive development targets, creation challenges, and the straightforward idea of Chief Elon Musk have drawn in examination. Work rehearses at Tesla's manufacturing plants, worries over work environment security, and claims of association busting have brought up moral issues about the organization's tasks. The instability of Tesla's stock, affected by hypothesis and market feeling, has added intricacy to its account.

The worldwide idea of Tesla's tasks, especially its venture into the Chinese market, features the complexities of working in a complicated and interconnected world. While Tesla has made huge progress in China, turning into a central part on the planet's biggest auto market, it has needed to explore moves going from exchange pressures to quality control issues. The experience highlights the sensitive interaction between financial, political, and social factors that shape the scene for maintainable innovation organizations working on a worldwide scale.

9.3 Closing thoughts on the lasting legacy of "Tesla's Drive."

In considering the enduring tradition of "Tesla's Drive," one is constrained to recognize the significant effect this imaginative organization has had on molding the direction of various ventures and affecting cultural viewpoints on supportability. Past the domain of electric vehicles, Tesla's heritage is a story of brassy objectives, mechanical development, and a tenacious obligation to speeding up the world's change to feasible energy.

Tesla's drive isn't simply a significant motto yet a demonstration of the vision and assurance of its pioneer, Elon Musk. At the center of Tesla's heritage is Musk's steadfast faith in the basic of progressing to economical energy sources. Musk's daring objectives, from changing the car business to colonizing Mars, have risen above the limits of ordinary reasoning, motivating both esteem and doubt. However, unequivocally this strength has moved Tesla into the vanguard of organizations driving groundbreaking change.

The car scene, when overwhelmed by gas powered motors, has seen a seismic shift because of "Tesla's Drive." The presentation of the Tesla Roadster in 2008 denoted the start of another time, dissipating the idea that electric vehicles were restricted to drowsy, specialty markets. Tesla's obligation to creating electric vehicles that matched as well as outperformed their conventional partners in execution, reach, and allure modified customer discernments. The ensuing models — Model S, Model 3, Model X, and Model Y — set Tesla's situation as a main impetus in the car business.

Tesla's impact reaches out past its own piece of the pie, igniting a flood of rivalry and development in the car area. Customary automakers, at first reluctant to put resources into electric vehicle innovation, have been constrained to recalibrate their methodologies in light of Tesla's prosperity. The outcome has been an expansion of electric vehicle contributions from laid out automakers, extending purchaser decisions and speeding up the progress to feasible transportation on a worldwide scale.

Essential to Tesla's inheritance is its commitment to reshaping public arrangement and industry elements. State run administrations around the world, perceiving the natural advantages of electric vehicles, have sanctioned strategies boosting their reception. Appropriations, tax reductions, and discharges guidelines have been made to urge customers and organizations to embrace clean energy arrangements. Tesla's outcome in exhibiting the suitability of electric vehicles as a standard choice plays had an essential impact in forming these strategy scenes and cultivating an administrative climate helpful for feasible development.

Nonetheless, Tesla's effect isn't bound to the car area. The organization's introduction to environmentally friendly power arrangements and energy stockpiling highlights a comprehensive way to deal with supportability. The securing of SolarCity in 2016 denoted Tesla's essential passage into the sun powered energy market.

The Sun powered Rooftop, a consistent joining of sun based tiles with customary roofing materials, epitomizes Tesla's obligation to creative arrangements that reach out past transportation. By enhancing into sunlight based energy and energy stockpiling, Tesla positions itself as an extensive clean energy organization, adding to the more extensive objective of a maintainable energy future.

Energy capacity arrangements, including the Powerwall, Powerpack, and Megapack, address one more component of Tesla's enduring heritage. These capacity arrangements assume a critical part in improving the dependability and security of sustainable power sources. The capacity to store overabundance energy created during top creation periods and delivery it during seasons of popularity tends to one of the critical difficulties of environmentally friendly power - irregularity. Tesla's energy stockpiling advancements contribute not exclusively to individual buyers yet in addition to the versatility and maintainability of whole energy networks.

Tesla's obligation to vertical coordination, typified by the Gigafactories decisively situated across the globe, is a sign of its enduring inheritance. These gigantic offices, devoted to in-house creation of batteries and electric drivetrains, connote a takeoff from customary assembling models. The Gigafactory idea permits Tesla to accomplish economies of scale, smooth out creation processes, and apply more prominent command over key parts' quality and cost. This upward coordination is key to Tesla's capacity to increase creation, diminish expenses, and advance battery innovation.

Key to the enduring tradition of "Tesla's Drive" is the effect on cultural insights and purchaser conduct. Tesla's electric vehicles are not only methods of transportation; they are images of advancement, extravagance, and natural cognizance. The optimistic allure of Tesla's vehicles, joined with their elite exhibition and state of the art innovation, plays had a significant impact in normalizing electric vehicles as attractive and standard. Tesla has figured out how to transform manageability into a selling point, dissipating the thought that eco-accommodating decisions accompany splits the difference in execution or style.

However, similarly as with any groundbreaking excursion, Tesla's inheritance isn't without its difficulties and contentions. The organization's aggressive development targets, creation difficulties, and Chief Elon Musk's candid correspondence style have been subjects of investigation. Moral worries connected with work rehearses, working environment wellbeing, and claims of association busting have brought up issues about the moral elements of Tesla's tasks. The instability of Tesla's stock, impacted by market hypothesis and opinion, adds a layer of intricacy to its story.

The worldwide development of Tesla's tasks, especially its progress in the Chinese market, epitomizes the intricacies of working in a world interconnected by monetary, political, and social powers. While Tesla has made huge progress in China, turning into a key part in the biggest auto market universally, it has explored moves going from exchange pressures to quality control issues. This worldwide experience highlights the mind boggling interchange of variables that shape the scene for economical innovation organizations working on a worldwide scale.